Arapahoe County, Colorado Territory Criminal Court Index

1862–1879

An Annotated Index

Compiled by Dina C. Carson

Arapahoe County, Colorado Territory Criminal Court Index 1862–1879

An Annotated Index

Compiled by Dina C. Carson

Published by:

Iron Gate Publishing
P.O. Box 999
Niwot, CO 80544

Printed in the United States of America

	ISBN	1-879579-70-7	ISBN 13	978-1-879579-70-5
eBook	ISBN	1-879579-69-3	ISBN 13	978-1-879579-69-9

Introduction

The Arapahoe County, Colorado Territory Criminal Court Index 1862-1879 contains an alphabetical list of criminal cases filed by the name of the first defendant listed on the case.

It gives the date of filing, the case number, the charge, the book and page number of subsequent hearings, and a brief description of the findings of those hearings. Often, the dispensation of the case will be given in the notes.

The very early cases, listed as occuring "bef 1862," have no actual dates on the case but occur in the order of cases before others prosecuted in late 1862. These early cases being prosecuted as The People of the United States of America vs the defendant, and were probably in the jurisdiction of the US Marshals. Most of these cases are listed as Treason, etc., most likely cases of Southern sympathizers as the Civil War was underway.

It appears that the courts had their hands full with notorious saloon-owning brothers Edward and John Chase, not to mention forgers and miners passing off counterfeit gold dust.

The Arapahoe County Criminal Court Index is held by the Colorado State Archives and is accessible for research. You can order a copy of pages from the *Arapahoe County Criminal Court Index, 1862-1879* by calling the Colorado State Archives or placing an order through their website.

Abner, Louis
1872 Oct 10, Case No. 525 -
Larceny; 1873 Apr 9, Case No.
669 - Burglary; 1877 Sept 11, Case
No. 1139 - Larceny

Achy, James
1864 Apr 7, Case No. 138 -
Larceny

Adams, Charles
1878 Jan 10, Case No. 1164 -
Burglary

Adams, John
1878 Sept 9, Case No. 1245 -
Forgery; 1878 Sept 9, Case No.
1246 - Forgery; 1878 Sept 9, Case
No. 1247 - Forgery

Adams, Lorenzo D
1879 Jan 31, Case No. 1235 -
Contempt

Adler, Mesco
bef 1862, Case No. 1 - Wilful
Murder

Adobe Moll
1876 Sept 5, Case No. 965 - alias
of Mary Gallagher; 1876 Sept
14, Case No. 990 - alias for Mary
Gallagher; 1877 Jan 18, Case No.
1035 - alias of Mary Gallagher

Aduddell, Robert G
1871 June 21, Case No. 470 -
Manslaughter; 1871 June 21, Case
No. 471 - Manslaughter

Aikens, Dennis
1873 May 10, Case No. 602 -
Contempt

Aikens, John
1873 May 10, Case No. 601 -
Contempt

Aikens, Joseph J
1876 Sept 5, Case No. 929 -
Larceny; 1876 Sept 5, Case No.
930 - Forgery

Alberton, Edward
1871 June 15, Case No. 468 -
Larceny

Alberton, Willis
1873 Apr 11, Case No. 540 -
Larceny

Alden, John
1878 Jan 14, Case No. 1179 -
Larceny

Alister, J B
1877 Jan 26, Case No. 1046 -
Contempt

Allen, Andrew
1864 Apr 13, Case No. 145 -
Gambling

Allen, John
1879 Apr 15, Case No. 1343 -
Threats

Allison, Frank
1878 Apr 10, Case No. 1208 -
Threats

Anderson, Arthur
1871 Oct 21, Case No. 488 - Murder

Anderson, James
1867 Dec 11, Case No. 343 - Larceny

Anderson, William C
1875 Sept 30, Case No. 751 - Appeal

Angel, George
1877 Jan 12, Case No. 998 - Embezzlement

Annabil, Arthur E et al
1877 Apr 26, Case No. 1086 - Larceny; 1877 Apr 26, Case No. 1087 - Larceny; 1877 Apr 26, Case No. 1088 - Larceny; 1877 Apr 26, Case No. 1089 - Larceny; 1877 Apr 26, Case No. 1090 - Larceny; 1877 Apr 26, Case No. 1091 - Larceny; 1877 Apr 26, Case No. 1092 - Larceny; 1877 Apr 26, Case No. 1093 - Larceny; 1877 Apr 26, Case No. 1094 - Larceny; 1877 Apr 26, Case No. 1095 - Larceny; 1877 Apr 26, Case No. 1096 - Larceny; 1877 Apr 26, Case No. 1097 - Larceny; 1877 Apr 26, Case No. 1098 - Larceny

Arant, Joseph
1866 Dec 6, Case No. 264 - Larceny

Arbor, Albert
1870 Jan 20, Case No. 397 - Keeping Gaming Tenement; 1870 Jan 20, Case No. 398 - Keeping Gaming Tables; 1870 Jan 20, Case No. 401 - Keeping Gambling House; 1870 June 20, Case No. 413 - Keeping Gambling Tenement; 1866 Dec 14, Case No. 289 - Keeping Gambling Room

Ardinger, H D
1866 Dec 12, Case No. 284 - Larceny

Armstrong, J W
1877 May 17, Case No. 1110 - Contempt

Armstrong, John
1879 Apr 21, Case No. 1347 - Larceny

Armstrong, Richard
1870 June 17, Case No. 411 - Larceny; 1870 June 17, Case No. 412 - Larceny

Arnett, George
1871 Oct 3, Case No. 491 - Contempt

Arnold, Tilghman
1873 Apr 11, Case No. 542 - Larceny; 1879 Apr 11, Case No. 543 - Larceny

Artliss, Homer
1878 Sept 9, Case No. 1248 - Assault

Ashar, Columbus
bef 1862, Case No. 50 - Treason etc.

Athey, James L
1877 Sept 7, Case No. 1121 - Larceny

Atkinson, Charles N
1877 Apr 24, Case No. 1078 - Forgery; 1877 Apr 24, Case No. 1079 - False Pretenses

Atkinson, William
1875 Sept 18, Case No. 814 - Larceny

Ayers, J E
1875 Oct 18, Case No. 850 - Contempt

Ayers, Jeremiah E
1876 May 27, Case No. 923 - Contempt

Ayers, Lee
1866 Mar 23, Case No. 231 - Gambling

Ayers, Thomas
bef 1862, Case No. 3 - no charge listed

Babcock, Andrew B
bef 1862, Case No. 80 - Grand Larceny

Babcock, George
1873 May 7, Case No. 598 - Contempt; 1878 Apr 20, Case No. 1221 - False Pretenses; 1878 Apr 20, Case No. 1222 - False Pretenses; 1878 Apr 20, Case No. 1223 - False Pretenses; 1878 Jan 15, Case No. 1193 - False Pretenses; 1878 Jan 15, Case No. 1194 - False Pretenses; 1878 Jan 15, Case No. 1195 - False Pretenses; 1878 Jan 15, Case No. 1196 - False Pretenses; 1878 Jan 15, Case No. 1197 - False Pretenses; 1878 Jan 15, Case No. 1198 - Larceny

Badelet, Clayton
bef 1862, Case No. 12 - alias of Clayton Scott

Baker, John
1875 Oct 26, Case No. 853 - Contempt

Ballotti, Michale
1876 Jan 28, Case No. 861 - Murder

Bank, Michael
bef 1862, Case No. 78 - Passing counterfeit gold dust

Banks, James M
bef 1862, Case No. 10 - Assault with a Deadly Weapon with Intent to Kill

Banks, John
1866 Mar 23, Case No. 232 - Larceny

Bannock, John
1873 Oct 9, Case No. 633 - False Pretenses

Barbero, Drusciano
1873 Sept 9, Case No. 629 - Larceny

Barker, Frank
1878 Apr 18, Case No. 1214 - Larceny

Barnes, O J
1877 Oct 5, Case No. 1159 - Contempt

Barnum, Charles
1870 June 20, Case No. 423 - Common Gambler

Barnumn, Charles
bef 1862, Case No. 8 - Assault with a Deadly Weapon; bef 1862, Case No. 9 - Larceny and Conspiracy

Barry, James
1877 Apr 23, Case No. 1057 - Forgery; 1877 Apr 23, Case No. 1058 - Forgery; 1877 Apr 23, Case No. 1059 - Forgery; 1877 Apr 23, Case No. 1060 - Forgery

Bartholomew, William
1872 Jan 4, Case No. 496 - Burglary

Bartlett, Charles L
1863 Mar 4, Case No. 111 - Malfeasance

Barton, E R
1876 Oct 30, Case No. 993 - Contempt

Barton, Elias R
1875 Jan 22, Case No. 860 - Contempt

Bateman, George
1878 Aug 28, Case No. 1238 - Threats

Bates, Joseph et all
1877 Dec 26, Case No. 1163 - Selling whiskey without a license

Bauer, Apollonia
1872 Oct 10, Case No. 518 - Larceny

Bauffman, Frederick
1865 Dec 20, Case No. 186 - Larceny

Baufman, Fred
1865 Dec 13, Case No. 157 - Larceny

Baxter, William
1878 Sept 9, Case No. 1249 - Larceny; 1878 Sept 9, Case No. 1250 - Larceny; 1878 Sept 9, Case No. 1251 - Larceny; 1878 Sept 9, Case No. 1252 - Larceny; 1878 Sept 9, Case No. 1253 - Larceny

Bazemen, Alex
1866 Mar 23, Case No. 230 - Gaming

Beal, Moses
1876 Jan 29, Case No. 871 - Larceny

Beals, Moses
1873 Oct 7, Case No. 607 - Burglary

Bean, John
1864 Apr 18, Case No. 142 - Gambling

Bear, Jacob E
1875 Apr 6, Case No. 753 -
Larceny

Beckwith, James P
bef 1865, Case No. 153 -
Manslaughter

Bedford, John
1874 Nov 3, Case No. 720 -
Burglary

Beeler, Fredericka
1873 Oct 11, Case No. 637 -
Forgery; 1874 Apr 9, Case No. 666
- Forgery

Begar, Richard
1877 July 12, Case No. 1120 -
Contempt

Bell, Charles
1873 Apr 11, Case No. 547 -
Burglary

Bell, Jasper C
bef 1862, Case No. 40 - Treason,
etc.

Bell, Thaddeus P
bef 1862, Case No. 20 - Treason
etc.

Beller, Charles
1878 Sept 13, Case No. 1272 -
Disturbing the Peace

Bennalli, Joseph
1876 Sept 13, Case No. 982 -
Accessory after the fact to murder

Bennett, Charles C
1871 June 15, Case No. 466 -
Murder

Benton, Jesse
1870 Jan 20, Case No. 402 -
Common Gambler; 1870 Jan 20,
Case No. 403 - Common Gambler;
1870 June 20, Case No. 421 -
Common Gambler

Berkley, Junius
1867 Dec 2, Case No. 321 -
Murder

Bettley, Stephen
1878 Apr 8, Case No. 1209 -
Threats

Bilch, Frank
1871 Oct 4, Case No. 480 - Assault
with Intent to Kill

Bill, Francis R
1864 Apr 7, Case No. 132 -
Embezzlement

Blair, Edward
1878 Jan 14, Case No. 1180 -
Robbery

Blake, Isaac E
1876 Oct 30, Case No. 993 -
Contempt

Blake, Orris
1874, Case No. 687 - Contempt

Bledsoe, Chas
1866 Mar 24, Case No. 248 -
Larceny

Bluen, Mary
bef 1865, Case No. 152 - Larceny

Blume, Charles H
1878 Jan 10, Case No. 1166 -
Larceny; 1878 Jan 10, Case No.
1167 - Larceny; 1878 Jan 10, Case
No. 1168 - Bigamy; 1878 Jan 14,
Case No. 1181 - Bigamy

Boldt, John
1878 Jan 10, Case No. 1169 -
Larceny

Bolochied, A
1875 June 8, Case No. 810 -
Contempt

Bond, William S
bef 1862, Case No. 69 - Passing
counterfeit gold dust

Booth, George
bef 1862, Case No. 16 - Larceny;
bef 1862, Case No. 22 - Treason,
etc.

Borden, Charles
1879, Case No. 1344 - Burglary;
1879 Apr 21, Case No. 1344 -
Threats

Borley, George
bef 1862, Case No. 76 - Passing
counterfeit gold dust

Born, Charles
1873 Mar 26, Case No. 538 -
Appeal

Born, Gus N
1872 Oct 10, Case No. 516 -
Larceny

Bouacina, George W
1871 Jan 7, Case No. 446 - Forgery

Bowen, Fensuto F
1878 Apr 18, Case No. 1213 -

Bowen, James
1877 Jan 12, Case No. 1000 -
Larceny

Bowerman, Richard
1876 Apr 26, Case No. 927 -
Contempt

Bowers, Edward
1868 May 6, Case No. 348 -
Larceny

Bowers, Joseph H
1875 May 20, Case No. 812 -
Contempt

Boyce, James
1871 Oct 21, Case No. 488 -
Murder; 1877 Sept 1, Case No.
1153 - Threats; 1879 Apr 8, Case
No. 1339 - Threats

Boyd, William
1871 Jan 7, Case No. 447 - Larceny

Boyle, Charles
1877 Feb 19, Case No. 1038 -
Perjury

Boyle, Eugene
1877 Jan 18, Case No. 1027 -
Larceny

Boyle, Sarah J
1877 Feb 19, Case No. 1039 -
Perjury

Boyle, Timothy
1877 Jan 18, Case No. 1027 -
Larceny

Brackett, Edwd H
1865 Dec 20, Case No. 183 -
Forgery

Bradford, Robert B
1868 Oct 9, Case No. 356 - Assault
with Intent to Kill

Bradley, James M
bef 1862, Case No. 43 - Treason,
etc.

Bradley, James N
bef 1862, Case No. 38 - Treason,
etc.

Bradshaw, Alexander B
bef 1862, Case No. 29 - Treason,
etc.

Bradshaw, Robert
1876 Jan 29, Case No. 870 -
Larceny

Brady, Charles
1873 Oct 8, Case No. 618 -
Larceny

Branaman, John
bef 1862, Case No. 11 - Murder

Brandenburg, Alexander
1875 Oct 8, Case No. 846 -
Contempt

Brendlinger, Hiram J
1871 June 15, Case No. 472 -
Contempt

Brett, James
1869 Jan 21, Case No. 370 -
Larceny

Brewster, Allen
1872 Oct 10, Case No. 520 -
Larceny

Brigg, Harvey
bef 1862, Case No. 48 - Treason,
etc.

Bristol, George
1870, Case No. 427 -

Britt, James
1869 Jan 21, Case No. 367 -
Larceny; 1869 Jan 21, Case No.
368 - Larceny

Broad, Wilmot E
1874 Sept 17, Case No. 703 -
Larceny

Brocade, Phillip
1867 Dec 9, Case No. 333 -
Larceny

Brokaw, Addie
1874 Apr 10, Case No. 679 -
Adultery

Bromfartner, Max
1862 Aug 26, Case No. 88 - Arson

Brown, A G
1872 Aug 31, Case No. 513 -
Appeal

Brown, Abraham C
bef 1862, Case No. 51 - Treason, etc.

Brown, Albert G
1873 Oct 7, Case No. 616 - Larceny

Brown, Charles
1865 Dec 15, Case No. 168 - Larceny

Brown, Charles W
1879 Jan 13, Case No. 1315 - Assault

Brown, Frank
1866 Mar 23, Case No. 233 - Gambling; 1866 Mar 23, Case No. 234 - Gambling

Brown, George
bef 1862, Case No. 4 - Larceny, Receiving Stolen Goods, alias Joseph Brown

Brown, George
1872 Jan 4, Case No. 495 - Assault with intent to kill and murder

Brown, Isaac
1874 Oct 14, Case No. 739 - Contempt; 1874 Oct 15, Case No. 732 - Keeping Gambling Room

Brown, Joseph
bef 1862, Case No. 4 - alias of George Brown

Brown, P T
1876 Sept 5, Case No. 943 - Threats

Brown, Samuel C
1877 Sept 11, Case No. 1135 - Assault

Brown, Theodore
1873 Apr 14, Case No. 576 - Aiding in keeping and exhibiting gaming tables

Bruban, Steven
1879 Jan 6, Case No. 1288 - Threats

Bryant, George N
1863 Nov 5, Case No. 127 - Perjury

Bucher, Eli
1871 June 15, Case No. 460 - Felonious Assault

Buckner, Felix
1866 Dec 8, Case No. 278 - Assault with Intent to Kill

Buford, Charles
bef 1862, Case No. 15 - Larceny and Receiving Stolen Goods, alias Texas; bef 1862, Case No. 17 - Burglary, alias Texas

Bull, H S
1873 May 3, Case No. 594 - Contempt

Burger, Thomas
1874 Apr 8, Case No. 649 - Larceny

Burke, Peter
1863 Mar 3, Case No. 100 - Riot

Burke, Peter
1863 Mar 3, Case No. 104 -
Larceny

Burke, Robert
1875 Sept 25, Case No. 840 -
Assault with intent to kill

Burnett, George
1877 May 23, Case No. 1115 -
Contempt

Burns, David
1870 Oct 8, Case No. 438 -
Larceny

Burns, Frank
1879 Jan 13, Case No. 1314 -
Disturbing the Peace

Burns, John
1875 Apr 9, Case No. 770 -
Larceny

Burns, Thomas
1878 Sept 9, Case No. 1239 -
Arson

Buschspio, Keury B
1866 Dec 14, Case No. 290 -
Larceny

Bushee, William H
1865 Dec 16, Case No. 174 -
Assault with intent to commit rape

Butler, Charles
1877 Sept 11, Case No. 1140 -
Larceny

Butler, Simon
1866 Mar 27, Case No. 255 -
Larceny

Butler, Thomas
1878 Jan 10, Case No. 1165 -
Burglary

Butler, Wm
1878 May 6, Case No. 1227 -
Contempt

Buzzard, William W
1866 Mar 22, Case No. 259 -
Appeal

Cady, Margaret E
bef 1862, Case No. 6 - Larceny &
Receiving Stolen Goods

Calbrut, Jno
1889 Apr 21, Case No. 1358 -
Burglary

Caldwell, Thomas
1876 Apr 13, Case No. 895 -
Adultery & Fornication

Calis, William A
1877 Jan 13, Case No. 1011 -
Appeal

Calvert, Martine
1879 Apr 21, Case No. 1349 -
Malicious Mischief

Cameron, Allen
1867 June 13, Case No. 298 -
Larceny

Cameron, John
1876 Jan 29, Case No. 872 -
Larceny

Campbell, Andrew
1877 Sept 7, Case No. 1122 -
Forgery

Campbell, Stewart
bef 1862, Case No. 14 - Larceny

Campbell, Thomas
1866 Dec 6, Case No. 261 -
Robbery

Campbell, William
1877 Jan 18, Case No. 1028 -
Larceny

Campbell, William A
1875 Apr 6, Case No. 755 -
Larceny

Cannady, John
1872 Oct 10, Case No. 528 -
Common Gambler

Carr, Edward
1867 Dec 4, Case No. 324 -
Robbery

Carr, William
1866 Dec 12, Case No. 279 -
Larceny

Cartwright, R H
1875 Oct 26, Case No. 852 -
Contempt

Cary, John
1869 Oct 7, Case No. 396 -
Larceny

Case, John M
1877 Apr 24, Case No. 1080 - False
Pretenses

Case, Mary M
1877 Apr 24, Case No. 1080 - False
Pretenses

Casey, John
1870 Oct 8, Case No. 432 -
Robbery

Cavanaugh, Jennie
1876 Apr 18, Case No. 894 -
Assault with a deadly weapon

Cavenaugh, John
1866 Dec 14, Case No. 291 -
Larceny

Cavenaugh, Peter
1878 Sept 9, Case No. 1241 -
Cruelty to animals

Chamberlin, George
bef 1862, Case No. 30 - Treason
etc.

Chamberlin, W H
1876 Apr 13, Case No. 897 -
Forgery

Champion, Benj
1867 June 17, Case No. 313 -

Chapman, Luie
1879 Jan 8, Case No. 1298 -
Threats

Charpiot, Jacob
1867 June 20, Case No. 319 -
Appeal

Charpiot, Jacques
1876 Sept 5, Case No. 946 -
Threats

Chase, Edward
bef 1862, Case No. 9 - Larceny
and Conspiracy; 1864 Apr 11,
Case No. 140 - Keeping Gambling

House; 1866 Mar 20, Case No. 195 - Gambling; 1866 Mar 20, Case No. 196 - Gambling; 1866 Mar 20, Case No. 197 - Gambling; 1866 Mar 20, Case No. 198 - Displaying Gaming Establishment and Gambling; 1866 Mar 21, Case No. 202 - Keeping Gambling House; 1866 Mar 21, Case No. 203 - Keeping Gambling House; 1866 Mar 21, Case No. 205 - Gambling; 1866 Mar 21, Case No. 215 - Gambling; 1866 Mar 22, Case No. 225 - Keeping Gambling House; 1866 Mar 22, Case No. 226 - Keeping Gambling House; 1866 Mar 22, Case No. 227 - Keeping Gambling House; 1866 Mar 22, Case No. 228 - Keeping Gambling House; 1866 Mar 22, Case No. 229 - Keeping Gambling House; 1866 Mar 27, Case No. 252 - Gambling; 1866 Mar 27, Case No. 253 - Gambling; 1867 Dec 9, Case No. 329 - no charge listed; 1867 Dec 9, Case No. 335 - Keeping Tenement Room for Gambling; 1867 Dec 9, Case No. 337 - Keeping Gambling Establishment; 1867 June 17, Case No. 314 - Keeping Gambling House; 1870 June 20, Case No. 417 - Keeping Gambling Room; 1871 June 15, Case No. 467 - Assault with intent to commit murder; 1872 Oct 11, Case No. 536 - Keeping Gambling Establishment; 1873 Apr 14, Case No. 561 - Keeping Gambling Room; 1873 Apr 14, Case No. 562 - Keeping Gambling Room; 1873 June 13, Case No. 591 - Contempt

Chase, John
1867 Dec 9, Case No. 334 - Keeping Gambling Establishment; 1867 Dec 9, Case No. 339 - Keeping Gambling Establishment; 1870 Jan 20, Case No. 399 - Keeping Gambling Tenement; 1870 Jan 20, Case No. 400 - Keeping Gaming Tables; 1870 Jan 20, Case No. 401 - Keeping Gambling House; 1870 June 20, Case No. 413 - Keeping Gambling Tenement; 1873 Apr 14, Case No. 548 - Keeping Gambling Room; 1873 Apr 14, Case No. 563 - Keeping Gambling Room; 1873 Apr 14, Case No. 564 - Keeping Gambling Room; 1873 Apr 14, Case No. 565 - Keeping Gambling Room; 1873 Apr 14, Case No. 566 - Keeping Gambling Room; 1873 Apr 14, Case No. 567 - Keeping Gambling Room; 1873 Apr 14, Case No. 568 - Keeping Gambling Room; 1873 Apr 14, Case No. 569 - Keeping Gambling Room; 1873 Apr 14, Case No. 570 - Keeping Gambling Room; 1873 Apr 14, Case No. 571 - Keeping Gambling Room; 1873 Apr 14, Case No. 572 - Keeping Gambling Room; 1873 Apr 14, Case No. 573 - Keeping Gambling Room; 1873 Apr 14, Case No. 574 - Keeping Gambling Room; 1873 Apr 14, Case No. 575 - Keeping Gambling Room; 1873 June 13, Case No. 591 -

Contempt; 1873 Oct 7, Case No. 616 - Larceny

Chase, John et al
1873 Apr 11, Case No. 545 - Larceny

Cheeswright, Charles
1875 Dec 31, Case No. 859 - Appeal

Cheney, Parker B
1866 Mar 24, Case No. 246 - Gambling; 1866 Mar 24, Case No. 247 - Gambling

Cherat, Charles A
1877 Jan 12, Case No. 1001 - Forgery; 1877 Jan 12, Case No. 1002 - Forgery; 1877 Jan 12, Case No. 1003 - Forgery; 1877 Jan 12, Case No. 1004 - Forgery; 1877 Apr 23, Case No. 1061 - Forgery; 1877 Apr 23, Case No. 1062 - Forgery; 1877 Apr 23, Case No. 1063 - Forgery; 1877 Jan 12, Case No. 1005 - Forgery

Cherst, Charles L
1877 Apr 23, Case No. 1064 - no charges listed; 1877 Apr 23, Case No. 1065 - Forgery

Chervring, Thomas
bef 1862, Case No. 46 - Treason etc.

Chilton, John
1865 Dec 21, Case No. 194 - Larceny

Clancey, John
1864 Apr 7, Case No. 133 - Larceny

Clanton, Hiram R
bef 1862, Case No. 35 - Treason etc.

Clark, Charles
1874 Apr 8, Case No. 655 - Larceny

Clark, Emanuel
1867 Dec 9, Case No. 331 - Burglary

Clark, Francis D
1877 May 25, Case No. 1116 - Contempt

Clark, King
1877 Apr 21, Case No. 1048 - Larceny; 1877 Jan 15, Case No. 1012 - no charge listed

Clark, Mary A E
1873 Oct 10, Case No. 635 - Assault with intent to kill and murder

Clark, R M
1874 May 25, Case No. 691 - Contempt

Claudius, August
1873 Apr 14, Case No. 586 - Gambling

Cleary, Nicholas F
1879 Jan 15, Case No. 1329 - False Pretenses; 1879 Jan 15, Case No. 1330 - Forgery

Clinton, George
1874 Nov 30, Case No. 723 -
Robbery

Clinton, John
1866 Mar 22, Case No. 218 -
Burglary

Coburn, Paul
1867 June 14, Case No. 311 -
Larceny

Cochran, William
1874 Nov 30, Case No. 723 -
Robbery

Cochrane, Peter
1878 Jan 6, Case No. 1289 -
Threats

Cohn, Leopold
1874 May 12, Case No. 686 -
Contempt

Colburn, Burt
1878 Sept 9, Case No. 1240 -
Larceny

Colby, Abram M
bef 1862, Case No. 85 - Bribery

Cole, George
1870 June 20, Case No. 426 -
Keeping Gambling Room; 1878
Jan 14, Case No. 1182 - Larceny

Cole, Jerome
1875 Apr 8, Case No. 762 -
Larceny; 1875 Apr 8, Case No. 763
- Larceny

Cole, L H
1875 Oct 26, Case No. 854 -
Contempt

Cole, Lyman H
1876 Apr 13, Case No. 898 -
Larceny; 1876 Apr 13, Case No.
899 - Larceny; 1876 Apr 13, Case
No. 900 - Larceny; 1876 Apr 13,
Case No. 901 - Larceny

Collier, Charles
1876 Apr 14, Case No. 914 -
Receiving stolen goods

Collins, Moses
1868 Oct 9, Case No. 359 -
Larceny

Collins, William
1879 Jan 13, Case No. 1300 -
Larceny

Connor, Charles
1876 Jan 29, Case No. 870 -
Larceny

Cook, Charles A
1863 Mar 5, Case No. 113 -
Misdemeanor

Cook, Charles A et al
1877 Sept 12, Case No. 1150 - Riot

Cook, George
1871 June 15, Case No. 464 -
Larceny

Cook, Milton
1876 Apr 13, Case No. 907 - Riot

Cook, Vining
1867 June 14, Case No. 299 - Larceny

Coombs, John
1866 Dec 14, Case No. 296 - Larceny

Cooper, Arthur B
1877 Jan 12, Case No. 995 - Larceny

Cooper, Thomas
1872 Jan 4, Case No. 495 - Assault with intent to kill and murder

Corbet, George H
1875 Apr 10, Case No. 784 - Having Keys in possession with intent etc.; 1876 Sept 13, Case No. 979 - Larceny; 1876 Sept 13, Case No. 980 - Larceny

Corbett, Warren J
1874 Oct 13, Case No. 727 - Assault with intent to rob

Corley, David
1866 Dec 6, Case No. 261 - Robbery

Corman, George
1867 June 14, Case No. 312 - Murder

Cosverty, James
bef 1862, Case No. 63 - Robbery

Cotrell, Edward
1873 Oct 7, Case No. 610 - Forgery

Cotton, Alfred
1875 Jan 26, Case No. 750 - Appeal

Courvoisier, A
1876 Sept 5, Case No. 932 - Unlawful taking of fish

Courvossier, C A
1874 Oct 16, Case No. 742 - Contempt

Cowan, James
bef 1862, Case No. 57 - Treason etc.

Cowan, James
bef 1862, Case No. 75 - Murder

Cowell, Enos
1865 Dec 20, Case No. 184 - Forgery

Cowen, E R
1874 May 18, Case No. 688 - Contempt

Cox, Alfred
1876 Jan 29, Case No. 873 - Burglary

Coyle, John J
1876 Sept 5, Case No. 931 - Assault with intent to kill

Craddock, James
1863 Nov 3, Case No. 121 - Larceny

Cramer, John
1875 Apr 6, Case No. 760 - Larceny

Crawford, Ed
1862 Nov 5, Case No. 98 - Larceny

Crawford, Wear
1877 Apr 21, Case No. 1047 - False Pretenses

Crofton, Newton
1865 Dec 20, Case No. 190 - Larceny; 1865 Dec 20, Case No. 191 - Larceny; 1865 Dec 20, Case No. 192 - Larceny

Cronin, James
1875 Apr 6, Case No. 754 - Forgery

Crowley, Jerre
1875 Apr 10, Case No. 785 - Riot

Crowley, Jerry
1872 Oct 10, Case No. 526 - Common Gambler; 1877 Sept 11, Case No. 1140 - Larceny

Crump, John
1876 Sept 5, Case No. 944 - Threats

Culbert, William
1878 Apr 30, Case No. 1229 - Contempt

Cummins, Alvin
1877 Sept 11, Case No. 1137 - Malicious Mischief

Cunningham, Val J
1874 Apr 8, Case No. 664 - Larceny

Curley, John
1878 Sept 9, Case No. 1254 - Disturbing the Peace

Curley, John
1878 Sept 9, Case No. 1255 - Disturbing the Peace

Curtice, Lewis A
1878 Apr 23, Case No. 1228 - Contempt

Curtis, Lewis
1874 Oct 15, Case No. 732 - Keeping Gambling Room

Cutter, Charles
1874 Aug 19, Case No. 700 - Larceny Appeal

Cutter, Lorin W
1865 Dec 4, Case No. 164 - Larceny

Dailey, Peter et al
bef 1862, Case No. 118 -

Dailey, William
1873 Apr 14, Case No. 559 - Playing at game for money

Darlington, Richard D
1867 Sept 24, Case No. 320 - Murder

Dashmer, Francis
1865 Dec 16, Case No. 177 - Murder

Davidson, Daniel
1878 Dec 3, Case No. 1287 - Murder

Davidson, Isaac
1878 Feb 5, Case No. 1205 - Contempt

Davidson, John
1877 Sept 7, Case No. 1128 - Larceny

Davis, J C
1866 Dec 6, Case No. 266 - Larceny

Davis, James
1866 Dec 9, Case No. 330 - Gambling

Davis, John
1866 Dec 8, Case No. 268 - Assault with intent to commit rape; 1866 Dec 8, Case No. 269 - Assault with intent to commit rape; 1873 Apr 14, Case No. 559 - Playing at game for money; 1873 Apr 14, Case No. 588 - Gambling; 1873 Apr 14, Case No. 589 - Keeping Gambling Room; 1873 Apr 14, Case No. 590 - Keeping Gambling Room

Davis, Joseph C
1874 Sept 17, Case No. 703 - Larceny

Davis, Samuel S
1876 Sept 4, Case No. 948 - Threats; 1876 Sept 5, Case No. 949 - Threats

Dawson, John
1874 Apr 8, Case No. 659 - Larceny

Dawson, Samuel
bef 1862, Case No. 76 - Passing counterfeit gold dust; bef 1862, Case No. 86 - Passing counterfeit gold dust

Dean, Charles
1872 Apr 3, Case No. 503 - Larceny

DeLand, Abram
1871 Jan 7, Case No. 449 - Larceny; 1871 Jan 7, Case No. 450 - False Pretenses

Delaney, Peter
1876 Sept 5, Case No. 933 - Larceny

Deodata, Leonardo
1876 Jan 28, Case No. 861 - Murder; 1876 Sept 13, Case No. 983 - Accesory after the fact to murder; 1876 Sept 13, Case No. 984 - Accesory after the fact to murder

Deuel, Sarah J
1877 May 8, Case No. 1107 - Contempt

Devine, H S
1879 Jan 13, Case No. 1306 - Larceny

Devlin, James
1876 July 20, Case No. 928 - Appeal

Dewitt, William R
bef 1862, Case No. 93 -

Diamond, Daniel
1876 Jan 28, Case No. 869 -
Larceny

Dickson, T Lee
1874 Apr 9, Case No. 771 -
Burglary

Dickson, T Lee
1875 Apr 9, Case No. 772 -
Burglary; 1875 Apr 9, Case No.
773 - Larceny; 1875 Apr 9, Case
No. 774 - Burglary; 1875 Apr 9,
Case No. 775 - Burglary; 1875 Apr
9, Case No. 776 - Burglary; 1875
Apr 9, Case No. 777 - Larceny;
1875 Apr 9, Case No. 778 -
Burglary

Dickson, William
1875 Apr 9, Case No. 772 -
Burglary; 1875 Apr 9, Case No.
775 - Burglary; 1875 Apr 9, Case
No. 776 - Burglary; 1875 Apr 9,
Case No. 778 - Burglary

Diggs, Charles
1864 Apr 6, Case No. 130 -
Larceny

Diggs, Marion J
bef 1862, Case No. 47 - Treason
etc.

Dillon, Edward
1876 Sept 5, Case No. 947 -
Threats

Dillon, James
1879 Jan 6, Case No. 1290 -
Threats

Dillon, John
1863 Nov 5, Case No. 128 -
Larceny

Dimond, Daniel
1872 Apr 3, Case No. 502 -
Larceny; 1872 Apr 5, Case No. 507
- Assault with intent to kill and
murder; 1872 Apr 5, Case No. 509
- Escaping from jail

Doane, George
1873 Oct 10, Case No. 634 -
Larceny

Dodd, Francis
bef 1862, Case No. 61 - Assault
with intent to rob

Dodd, Robert
1875 Apr 6, Case No. 756 -
Larceny

Dodd, William
bef 1862, Case No. 61 - Assault
with intent to rob

Dodge, Frank
1871 June 15, Case No. 458 -
Forgery; 1871 June 15, Case No.
459 - Larceny

Dodge, L P
1877 Apr 23, Case No. 1066 - False
pretenses

Doe, John
1878 Jan 15, Case No. 1192 - Riot

Dolan, John
1876 Sept 6, Case No. 968 -
Malicious Mischief

Donacious, Barbers
1873 Oct 9, Case No. 629 -
Larceny

Donahue, Andrew
1877 Jan 12, Case No. 1000 -
Larceny

Donnell, Joseph
1874 Sept 17, Case No. 706 -
Larceny

Donnelly, Peter
1874 Apr 8, Case No. 652 -
Larceny; 1874 Apr 8, Case No. 657
- Larceny

Donnelly, Thomas
1864 Apr 7, Case No. 137 -
Larceny

Dore, Lillian
1879 Apr 21, Case No. 1348 -
Larceny

Doughnitz, Daniel
1871 May 29, Case No. 455 -
Administering drugs to procure
abortion

Douglas, H T
1866 Dec 14, Case No. 294 -
Larceny

Douglas, K T
1866 Dec 12, Case No. 284 -
Larceny

Downen, Alfred
1865 Dec 21, Case No. 193 -
Murder

Downen, Allen H
1872 Oct 10, Case No. 522 -
Larceny

Drane, G L
1871 Oct 10, Case No. 489 -
Contempt

Dugan, John
1873 Nov 29, Case No. 641 -
Assault & Battery

Duggan, James
1876 Sept 8, Case No. 971 -
Cruelty to animals

Duggan, Michael
1875 Apr 8, Case No. 765 -
Larceny

Duggy, Barney
1875 Sept 18, Case No. 815 -
Burglary

Duncan, Merrick
1874, Case No. 698 - Contempt

Dunham, Wright
1878 Sept 9, Case No. 1256 -
Murder

Dunn, ___
1875 Sept 18, Case No. 826 -
Larceny; 1875 Sept 18, Case No.
827 - Larceny

Dunn, Edward
1877 Apr 23, Case No. 1067 -
Forgery

Duval, Claude
1875 Apr 8, Case No. 764 -
Larceny

Eames, James K
1866 Mar 24, Case No. 244 - Gambling; 1866 Mar 24, Case No. 249 - Gambling

Easton, John S
bef 1862, Case No. 53 - Treason etc.

Eaton, James
1879 Jan 13, Case No. 1301 - Robbery

Eaton, William
1879 Jan 13, Case No. 1301 - Robbery

Eckels, Thomas
1876 Apr 13, Case No. 907 - Riot

Edis, Edward
1868 May 7, Case No. 352 - Fraudulent voting

Edwards, Henry
1878 Sept 13, Case No. 1274 - Larceny

Ehls, Adam
1877 Apr 24, Case No. 1081 - Larceny; 1877 Apr 24, Case No. 1082 - Larceny; 1877 Apr 24, Case No. 1083 - Larceny

Eitzen, C A
1873 May 26, Case No. 600 - Contempt

Elkins, John
1877 Apr 23, Case No. 1068 - Assault with intent to murder

Elkins, John
1877 Jan 12, Case No. 999 - Assault with a deadly weapon; 1877 Jan 15, Case No. 1013 - Adultery

Elliott, John
1877 Apr 27, Case No. 1106 - Contempt

Elliott, Joseph F
1867 June 13, Case No. 304 - Larceny

Elliott, Joshua
1867 June 17, Case No. 317 - Larceny

Elmore, Lafayette
bef 1862, Case No. 119 -

Elsner, John
1877 May 23, Case No. 1113 - Contempt

Elsner, Lena
1877 May 23, Case No. 1112 - Contempt

Emerson, Luther
1875 Apr 10, Case No. 786 - False Pretenses

Emmerson, James
1867 June 19, Case No. 316 - Keeping Gambling House; 1870 June 20, Case No. 416 - Keeping Gambling Room

Epps, Charles
1874 Sept 2, Case No. 713 - Burglary; 1874 Sept 23, Case No.

714 - Burglary; 1875 Apr 9, Case No. 779 - Larceny

Epstein, Isaac
1876 Sept 14, Case No. 989 - Arson

Epstein, Julius
1876 Sept 14, Case No. 989 - Arson

Estelle, John
1879 Apr 21, Case No. 1345 - Larceny

Evans, William
1876 Sept 4, Case No. 950 - Threats

Everett, Frank
1875 Apr 8, Case No. 885 - Obtaining money under false pretenses

Eyman, Charles
1879 Apr 21, Case No. 1350 - Assault

Fallen, Dennis
1869 May 4, Case No. 372 - Murder

Farley, Peter
1874 Aug 19, Case No. 700 - Larceny Appeal; 1874 May 5, Case No. 683 - Appeal

Fehan, James
1875 Apr 10, Case No. 785 - Riot

Felton, Rugus K
1869 May 7, Case No. 387 -

Ferguson, Charles B
1878 Sept 9, Case No. 1257 - Robbery

Fernandez, Henry
1876 Sept 13, Case No. 985 - Accessory after the fact to murder

Fernandez, Henry
1876 Sept 13, Case No. 986 - Accessory after the fact to murder

Fickler, George
1866 Dec 8, Case No. 276 - Manslaughter

Fields, Samuel
1875 Apr 6, Case No. 737 - Larceny

Fifield, J A
1875 Sept 21, Case No. 834 - Illegal Voting

Finerstein, Henry
1871 June 15, Case No. 469 - Riot

Fisher, Charles
1875 June 8, Case No. 811 - Contempt

Fisher, Jacob
1876 Apr 13, Case No. 902 - Forgery; 1876 Apr 13, Case No. 903 - Forgery; 1876 Apr 13, Case No. 904 - Forgery; 1876 Jan 29, Case No. 874 - Forgery; 1876 Jan 29, Case No. 875 - Forgery

Fisher, Orion A
bef 1862, Case No. 82 - Larceny

Fisher, Samuel H
1872 Apr 8, Case No. 506 -
Embezzlement

Fitzgerald, Patrick
1866 Mar 21, Case No. 199 -
Murder

Flacker, John
1869 May 6, Case No. 377 -
Larceny; 1869 May 6, Case No.
378 - Larceny

Flame, J
1879 Jan 13, Case No. 1301 -
Robbery

Flannagan, James
1867 June 13, Case No. 300 -
Larceny; 1867 June 13, Case No.
302 - Larceny

Flood, Peter
1863 Mar 3, Case No. 100 - Riot;
1863 Mar 3, Case No. 104 -
Larceny

Flynn, Edw
1871 Oct 4, Case No. 479 -
Robbery

Flynn, Thomas
1873 July 8, Case No. 603 - Assault
with intent to commit murder

Fogust, August
1869 May 7, Case No. 388 -
Larceny

Ford, Joseph M
1871 Jan 7, Case No. 452 - Assault
with intent to kill

Foster, Alvah D
1869 Apr 20, Case No. 371 -
Mayhem

Foster, Frank
1866 Mar 27, Case No. 250 -
Murder; 1866 Mar 27, Case No.
251 - Murder

Fourst, William
1865 Dec 15, Case No. 167 -
Larceny

Fowler, Lewis
1878 Sept 9, Case No. 1249 -
Larceny; 1878 Sept 9, Case No.
1250 - Larceny; 1878 Sept 9, Case
No. 1251 - Larceny; 1878 Sept 9,
Case No. 1252 - Larceny; 1878
Sept 9, Case No. 1253 - Larceny

Frain, Patrick
1877 Jan 15, Case No. 1014 -
Assault with a deadly weapon;
1878 Jan 10, Case No. 1170 -
Assault with a deadly weapon

Francis, Geo
1879 Jan 13, Case No. 1301 -
Robbery

Franke, Julius
1876 Apr 13, Case No. 905 -
Larceny; 1876 Jan 29, Case No.
876 - Burglary

Franklin, Louisa
1875 Sept 21, Case No. 835 -
Receiving stolen goods

Franklin, William
1867 Dec 4, Case No. 322 -

Larceny; 1867 Dec 4, Case No. 323 - Larceny

Fraser, R L
1876 June 30, Case No. 939 - Riot

Fraser, R S
1876 June 30, Case No. 951 - Threats

Fredendall, Arabella
1871 Jan 7, Case No. 446 - Forgery

Freeman, Henry
1872 May 18, Case No. 511 - Contempt

Freeman, John J
1874 Sept 17, Case No. 715 - Larceny

Fritsch, Frederick
1878 Jan 10, Case No. 1177 - Not a true bill

Frost, Frank
1873 Oct 8, Case No. 619 - Larceny

Frost, Jack
1879 Apr 21, Case No. 1351 - Assault

Fuller, Henry F
1874 Apr 8, Case No. 663 - Larceny

Gallagher, Mary
1876 Sept 14, Case No. 990 - Abduction, alias Adobe Moll; 1876 Sept 5, Case No. 965 - Abduction, alias Adobe Moll; 1877 Jan 18,

Case No. 1035 - Abducting, alias Adobe Moll

Galllimore, Frank
1865 Dec 14, Case No. 162 - Larceny

Gallotti, Philemona et al
1876 Jan 28, Case No. 861 - Murder; 1876 Jan 28, Case No. 862 - Murder; 1876 Jan 28, Case No. 863 - Murder; 1876 Jan 28, Case No. 864 - Murder; 1876 Jan 28, Case No. 865 - Murder; 1876 Jan 28, Case No. 866 - Murder; 1876 Jan 28, Case No. 867 - Murder; 1876 Jan 28, Case No. 868 - Murder; Gardner, Charles 1866 Mar 22, Case No. 220 - Gambling; 1876 Apr 14, Case No. 915 - Murder; 1876 Apr 14, Case No. 916 - Murder

Gardner, Charles
1866 Mar 22, Case No. 221 - Keeping Gaming House

Garland, Thomas
1874 Oct 13, Case No. 730 - Malicious Mischief

Garlinghouse, Lemuel
1866 Mar 24, Case No. 245 - Bigamy

Garner, John
1873 Apr 12, Case No. 553 - Larceny

Garvey, F F
1864 Apr 6, Case No. 131 - Larceny

Gates, Berry
1878 Sept 9, Case No. 1258 - Burglary

Gehon, Charles
1864 Apr 7, Case No. 148 - Peace warrant; 1864 Apr 7, Case No. 150 - Peace warrant

Geiger, Louis
1873 Oct 7, Case No. 611 - Larceny

Genboy, Charles
1877 Apr 23, Case No. 1069 - Assault with intent to murder

Geritt, Daniel K
bef 1862, Case No. 27 - Treason etc.

Gerrish, Joseph
1863 Nov 4, Case No. 125 - Larceny

Gerspach, John
1873 Nov 17, Case No. 640 - Threats

Gibbs, Elijah
1874 Sept 5, Case No. 701 - Murder (from Lake County)

Giddings, L A
1878 Feb 12, Case No. 1201 - Contempt

Gilchrist, James
1877 Sept 11, Case No. 1138 - Arson

Gildersleeve, George W
1877 May 18, Case No. 1111 - Contempt

Gildig, Julia
1874 Jan 9, Case No. 643 - Petit Larceny

Gile, Joseph F
1865 Dec 13, Case No. 156 - Assault with intent to kill

Gladfelty, Isaac
1875 May 1, Case No. 805 - Assault with intent to kill; 1875 May 10, Case No. 807 - Resisting an Officer

Glenmore, Zilla
1875 Apr 6, Case No. 758 - Larceny; 1875 May 1, Case No. 804 - Receiving stolen goods; 1875 Sept 18, Case No. 817 - Receiving stolen goods

Glick, Jerome S
bef 1862, Case No. 32 - Treason etc.

Glines, George
1874 Apr 11, Case No. 681 - False Pretenses

Goff, Mrs A J
1876 Sept 4, Case No. 945 - Threats

Golding, Phillip
1878 Feb 17, Case No. 1202 - Contempt

Gonzalez, Benito
1868 Oct 9, Case No. 360 -
Larceny; 1868 Oct 9, Case No. 362
- Larceny

Good, John
1871 June 15, Case No. 469 - Riot

Gossenier, Lucien
bef 1862, Case No. 62 - Larceny;
bef 1862, Case No. 65 - Assault
with intent to murder

Gotlieb, Joseph
1879 Jan 6, Case No. 1291 -
Threats

Gray, Vincent
bef 1862, Case No. 24 - Treason
etc.

Green, Charles
1876 Sept 8, Case No. 973 - False
Pretenses; 1876 Sept 9, Case No.
977 - False Pretenses

Greer, Mary A
1867 Dec 9, Case No. 340 -
Murder

Gregory, Jacob
1876 Apr 14, Case No. 917 -
Perjury

Gregory, John
1865 Dec 20, Case No. 189 -
Larceny

Griffin, John
1877 Sept 7, Case No. 1129 -
Disturbing the Peace

Griffin, Michael
1878 Apr 18, Case No. 1215 -
Burglary

Grifin, Henry
1879 Jan 13, Case No. 1316 -
Burglary

Griggs, Lafayette
1877 Sept 11, Case No. 1141 -
Larceny

Grimes, A C
1879 Jan 13, Case No. 1317 -
Assault

Grimet, Harry
1875 Sept 18, Case No. 816 -
Burglary, alias Harry Roberts;
1875 Sept 18, Case No. 821 - alias
of Harry Roberts; 1875 Sept 18,
Case No. 822 - alias of Harry
Roberts; 1875 Sept 18, Case No.
823 - alias of Harry Roberts; 1875
Sept 18, Case No. 824 - alias of
Harry Roberts

Griswold, J
1870 Oct 8, Case No. 439 - Murder

Gromm, F W
1878 Feb 5, Case No. 1206 -
Contempt

Groso, Julius
1876 Sept 8, Case No. 972 -
Larceny

Gross, Nathan
1869 Oct 7, Case No. 389 -
Burglary; 1869 Oct 7, Case No.

390 - Larceny; 1869 Oct 7, Case No. 391 - Larceny

Gross, Nathaniel
1867 Dec 9, Case No. 336 -

Guilford, James
1873 Oct 8, Case No. 623 - Larceny

Guion, George
1877 Sept 11, Case No. 1136 - Larceny

Hackney, Charles
1877 Jan 15, Case No. 1019 - Burglary

Hadley, A D
1866 Dec 14, Case No. 297 - Larceny

Hadley, Anderson D
1866 Mar 27, Case No. 254 - Larceny

Hadley, Joseph F
1866 Mar 27, Case No. 254 - Larceny

Hadley, Joseph H
1866 Dec 14, Case No. 297 - Larceny

Haetel, Frank
1875 Sept 25, Case No. 841 - Assault with a dangerous weapon

Haggerty, W J
1879, Case No. 1336 - Contempt

Hall, Benj F
1863 Mar 5, Case No. 112 - Palpable omission of duty

Hall, James
1875 Apr 6, Case No. 761 - Larceny

Halstead, Lewis
1864 Apr 7, Case No. 135 - Burglary & Larceny

Halyer, Watson
1879 Apr 15, Case No. 1340 - Threats

Hamilton, James
1876 Sept 4, Case No. 952 - Threats

Hamilton, Richard
1866 Dec 6, Case No. 265 - Assault with intent to kill

Hamilton, Robert
1872 Apr 18, Case No. 512 - Appeal

Hammann, John
1865, Case No. 161 - Perjury

Hammel, Ric
1870 May 20, Case No. 414 - Keeping Gambling Tenement

Hammel, Uriah
1866 Mar 21, Case No. 206 - Gambling; 1866 Mar 21, Case No. 207 - Gambling

Hammond, Kate
1877 Sept 11, Case No. 1142 - Larceny

Handin, Hattie
1874 Apr 10, Case No. 675 - Assault with intent to commit bodily injury

Haney, John
1866 Mar 21, Case No. 211 - Assault with intent to commit rape

Harman, Louis
1875 Apr 12, Case No. 799 - Assault & Battery with intent to murder

Harp, Clarence
1865 Dec 14, Case No. 163 - Larceny

Harrington, Wm D
1877 Sept 7, Case No. 1132 - Crime against nature

Harris, Daniel
1874 Apr 17, Case No. 722 - Burglary

Harris, Robert
1874 Sept 25, Case No. 708 - Burglary

Harris, Thomas
1872 Jan 4, Case No. 500 - Larceny

Harris, William
1871 Oct 15, Case No. 484 - Larceny; 1871 Oct 18, Case No. 485 - Larceny

Harris, William W
1875 Sept 18, Case No. 818 - Larceny

Harrison, Charles
bef 1862, Case No. 7 - Assault with a deadly weapon

Harrison, Henry
1864 Apr 6, Case No. 129 - Larceny

Harrison, James
1869 Jan 21, Case No. 366 - Larceny

Harrison, William
1875 Sept 21, Case No. 836 - Illegal voting; 1878 Sept 9, Case No. 1242 - Passing counterfeit money

Harshaw, Allen
1878 Jan 10, Case No. 1175 - Not a true bill

Hart, John
1867 Dec 9, Case No. 332 - Larceny

Hart, William
1868 Mar 6, Case No. 350 - Larceny

Hartman, George
1874 Apr 10, Case No. 678 - Assault with intent to Ravish

Harvey, Nicholas
1878 Jan 14, Case No. 1184 - Larceny

Harvey, Welford H
1867 June 14, Case No. 308 - Larceny

Hastings, Charles E
1879 Jan 13, Case No. 1305 - Burglary

Hastings, Samuel
1866 June 14, Case No. 301 - Larceny; 1867 June 13, Case No. 302 - Larceny

Hastings, Sarah
1873 Oct 14, Case No. 639 - Appeal

Haviland, William
1877 Apr 23, Case No. 1070 - Assault with intent to murder

Haxen, Nelson
bef 1862, Case No. 23 - Treason etc.

Hayes, James
1873 Oct 8, Case No. 620 - Larceny

Hays, George
1876 Apr 13, Case No. 898 - Larceny; 1876 Apr 13, Case No. 899 - Larceny; 1876 Apr 13, Case No. 900 - Larceny; 1876 Apr 13, Case No. 901 - Larceny

Hazlip, Bruce
1865 Dec 20, Case No. 178 - Larceny

Heath, William
1876 Apr 8, Case No. 887 - Larceny; 1876 Apr 8, Case No. 888 - Larceny; 1876 Apr 8, Case No. 889 - Larceny

Heatley, Francis P
1864 Apr 11, Case No. 140 - Keeping Gambling House; 1866 Mar 20, Case No. 195 - Gambling; 1866 Mar 20, Case No. 196 - Gambling; 1866 Mar 20, Case No. 197 - Gambling; 1866 Mar 20, Case No. 198 - Displaying Gaming Establishment and Gambling; 1866 Mar 21, Case No. 202 - Keeping Gambling House; 1866 Mar 21, Case No. 203 - Keeping Gambling House; 1866 Mar 21, Case No. 205 - Gambling; 1866 Mar 21, Case No. 215 - Gambling; 1866 Mar 22, Case No. 225 - Keeping Gambling House; 1866 Mar 22, Case No. 226 - Keeping Gambling House; 1866 Mar 22, Case No. 227 - Keeping Gambling House; 1866 Mar 22, Case No. 228 - Keeping Gambling House; 1866 Mar 22, Case No. 229 - Keeping Gambling House; 1866 Mar 27, Case No. 252 - Gambling; 1866 Mar 27, Case No. 253 - Gambling

Heiderer, William
1877 Jan 18, Case No. 1032 - Assault with a deadly weapon

Heiler, Frederick M
1878 Apr 18, Case No. 1216 - Assault with intent to murder

Helland, Joseph
1874 Apr 8, Case No. 658 - Larceny

Henderson, Albert
1878 Oct 15, Case No. 1284 -
Contempt

Henderson, John T
1875 Apr 9, Case No. 813 -
Contempt

Henderson, Peter
1879 Jan 13, Case No. 1304 -
Larceny

Hennessee, Michael
1871 Oct 15, Case No. 482 -
Gambling & Being Common
Gambler

Hensel, John
1878 Jan 10, Case No. 1174 - Not a
true bill

Herbert, Honora
1878 Aug 28, Case No. 1233 -
Threats

Herrick, Henry A
1868 May 6, Case No. 347 -
Larceny

Hessler, John
1874 Jan 12, Case No. 644 - Appeal

Hickey, William
1873 Apr 14, Case No. 577 -
Gambling

Hicklaw, James
1877 Sept 7, Case No. 1123 -
Larceny

Higgins, John
1871 Oct 4, Case No. 479 -
Robbery

Higgins, Patrick
1878 Jan 14, Case No. 1183 -
Selling obscene literature

Hildenburg, Henry
1872 Apr 3, Case No. 505 -
Larceny

Hill, A S
1876 Oct 30, Case No. 993 -
Contempt

Hill, Henry
1879 Jan 13, Case No. 1302 -
Robbery

Hill, James
1871 Oct 4, Case No. 478 - Murder

Hill, Myers
1864 Apr 7, Case No. 134 -
Larceny

Hiller, Charles
1872 Jan 4, Case No. 497 - Larceny

Hillgar, Elbert B
1869 Jan 21, Case No. 367 -
Larceny; 1869 Jan 21, Case No.
368 - Larceny; 1869 Jan 21, Case
No. 370 - Larceny

Hineley, Andrew
1876 Apr 13, Case No. 907 - Riot

Hines, Elmer R
1867 Dec 9, Case No. 340 -
Murder

Hinton, Robert
1877 Sept 7, Case No. 1131 -
Larceny

Hinton, S
1873 Apr 22, Case No. 593 -
Contempt

Hirst, William
1876 Sept 5, Case No. 935 -
Malicious Mischief

Hittson, John
1879 Jan 13, Case No. 1303 -
Assault with intent to murder;
1879 Jan 6, Case No. 1293 -
Threats

Hobson, James H
1876 Apr 8, Case No. 886 -
Embezzlement; 1876 Sept 4, Case
No. 934 - Embezzlement; 1877 Jan
18, Case No. 1029 - Larceny

Hoffman, Frank
1862 Aug 26, Case No. 87 -
Burglary

Hoffman, John
1876 June 30, Case No. 953 -
Assault

Hoffman, Katy
1876 June 30, Case No. 953 -
Assault

Hog, Theodore
1874 Jan 12, Case No. 644 - Appeal

Hogan, James
1879 Apr 21, Case No. 1352 -
Burglary

Hogan, Joseph
1876 Apr 13, Case No. 907 - Riot

Holly, Edward
1874 May 12, Case No. 686 -
Contempt; 1876 Sept 8, Case No.
974 - Embezzlement

Holtz, Edward
1875 Apr 8, Case No. 767 -
Larceny

Hoover, Jacob
1872 Oct 10, Case No. 519 -
Larceny

Hoover, Joseph
1865 Dec 20, Case No. 185 -
Larceny

Hopkins, Emma
1876 Apr 13, Case No. 907 - Riot

Horan, James
1875 Apr 9, Case No. 780 -
Robbery

Hordy, Alfred
1878 Jan 10, Case No. 1165 -
Burglary

Horey, Stephen
1867 June 14, Case No. 309 -
Larceny

Hosmer, Edward
1879 Jan 6, Case No. 1292 -
Threats

Hotson, James H
1877 Apr 21, Case No. 1049 -
Larceny

Houghton, Henry C
1875 Apr 12, Case No. 800 -

Obtaining money under false pretenses

Houghton, Henry M
1877 Feb 14, Case No. 1039 - Contempt

Houghton, Henry O
1875 Apr 10, Case No. 792 - False Pretenses

Houston, Mary
1878 Sept 9, Case No. 1259 - Assault

Houton, Henry O
1875 Apr 10, Case No. 791 - Cohabitation

Howard, Frank
1872 Oct 10, Case No. 523 - Larceny

Howard, Jennie
1878 Jan 14, Case No. 1189 - Not a true bill

Howland, W S
1878 Feb 12, Case No. 1200 - Contempt

Hudson, Stephen G
1874 Oct 1, Case No. 734 - Contempt; 1874 Oct 1, Case No. 735 - Contempt; 1874 Oct 7, Case No. 749 - Contempt

Huffman, John
1872 Apr 3, Case No. 504 - Assault with intent to kill and murder

Hughes, Charles C
1873 Apr 11, Case No. 550 - Manslaughter

Hughes, John
1878 Sept 9, Case No. 1260 - Larceny

Hughes, Thomas
1874 Apr 10, Case No. 677 - Assault with intent to rob

Hull, George
1872 Jan 4, Case No. 501 - Forfeiture of Recognizance

Hunt, George B
1869 Jan 21, Case No. 364 - Larceny; 1869 Jan 21, Case No. 369 - Larceny

Hynes, Maurice
1876 Apr 13, Case No. 904 - Forgery; 1876 Apr 13, Case No. 906 - Forgery

Irwin, Albert
1878 Jan 15, Case No. 1192 - Riot

Irwin, William
1879 Apr 21, Case No. 1353 - Assault

Irwin, William P
bef 1862, Case No. 18 - Treason etc.; bef 1862, Case No. 63 - Robbery

Israel, Milton N
1875 Apr 10, Case No. 787 - Assault with intent to kill

Ivory, John A
1879, Case No. 1337 - Contempt

Jackson, Edward
1872 Oct 10, Case No. 524 - Larceny

Jackson, George A
bef 1862, Case No. 5 - Assault with a Deadly Weapon with Intent to Kill; bef 1862, Case No. 34 - Treason etc.

James, William B
1866 Dec 6, Case No. 263 - Assault with intent to kill

Jamison, Henry W
1866 Dec 12, Case No. 281 - Larceny; 1866 Dec 12, Case No. 282 - Larceny

Jans, Peter
1873 Apr 10, Case No. 546 - Assault with intent to rape

Jelly, William
1870 June 20, Case No. 425 - Keeping Gambling Room

Jenkins, John
1865 Dec 16, Case No. 173 - Larceny

Jennie Big
1863 Mar 4, Case No. 110 - Keeping a Bawdy House

Jennings, Charlie
1872 Oct 10, Case No. 529 - Common Gambler

Johnson, Edward
1871 June 15, Case No. 461 - Larceny; 1874 Apr 10, Case No. 673 - Assault with intent to kill

Johnson, Henry
1870 Oct 8, Case No. 428 - Larceny

Johnson, James M
1872 Apr 12, Case No. 556 - Forgery; 1873 Apr 12, Case No. 555 - Forgery; 1873 Oct 7, Case No. 614 - Forgery; 1873 Oct 7, Case No. 615 - Forgery

Johnson, Robert E
bef 1862, Case No. 33 - Treason etc.

Johnson, Samuel
1873 Oct 7, Case No. 609 - Assault with intent to kill and murder

Johnson, Theodore H
bef 1862, Case No. 45 - Treason etc.; bef 1862, Case No. 63 - Robbery

Johnson, Theron W
1870, Case No. 427 -

Johnson, William
1866 Nov 6, Case No. 260 - Forgery; 1878 Apr 18, Case No. 1217 - Larceny

Johnston, John W
1875 May 10, Case No. 806 - Assault with intent to kill; 1875 May 10, Case No. 807 - Resisting an Officer

Jones, Daniel
1868 Oct 9, Case No. 358 - Larceny

Jones, H F
1878 Feb 8, Case No. 1203 - Contempt

Jones, James
1873 Oct 7, Case No. 613 - Larceny

Joslin, ___
1875 Sept 18, Case No. 826 - Larceny; 1875 Sept 18, Case No. 827 - Larceny

Judd, Charles P
1873 Oct 7, Case No. 608 - Larceny

Kalph, John
1877 Jan 18, Case No. 1034 - Larceny

Kane, Barney
1871 June 15, Case No. 463 - Assault with intent to kill

Keating, Jeff F
1872 Nov 15, Case No. 537 - Assault

Keefe, William
1875 Apr 6, Case No. 759 - Robbery

Keith, John
1863 Nov 4, Case No. 126 - Malfeasance

Keller, Dan
1872 Jan 4, Case No. 501 - Forfeiture of Recognizance

Kellog, Daniel Van
1869 May 6, Case No. 373 - Burglary

Kelly, John
1873 Oct 6, Case No. 604 - Burglary

Kelsey, Reuben
1862 Aug 26, Case No. 89 - Grand Larceny

Kemp, Thos
1867 June 19, Case No. 316 - Keeping Gambling House

Kennedy, Joseph L
1874 May 29', Case No. 692 - Contempt

Kennedy, William
1867 June 13, Case No. 302 - Larceny; 1867 June 14, Case No. 307 - Larceny

Kerr, Henry
1879 Jan 13, Case No. 1318 - Assault

Keyh, Alfred
1866 Dec 8, Case No. 271 - Larceny

King, Timothy
1868 Oct 9, Case No. 354 - Larceny

Kinncary, John P et al
1878 Jan 15, Case No. 1199 - Not a true bill

Kinnie, Victor
1866 Dec 6, Case No. 264 - Larceny

Kissig, Charles
1876 June 30, Case No. 956 - Threats

Klein, William R
1875 Apr 10, Case No. 788 - Abduction

Klemm, Richard
1877 Jan 18, Case No. 1030 - False Pretenses

Kline, Barney
1871 Oct 4, Case No. 477 - Larceny

Kline, Henry
1870 June 20, Case No. 420 - Keeping Gambling Tenement

Klotz, John
1869 May 7, Case No. 382 - Larceny; 1869 May 7, Case No. 383 - Receiving stolen goods

Klotze, John
1869 May 7, Case No. 381 - Larceny

Klotze, John M
1865 Dec 20, Case No. 179 - Larceny

Knowlen, Peter
1878 Jan 10, Case No. 1172 - Larceny

Koniberger, Otto
1876 Sept 8, Case No. 975 - Threats; 1876 Sept 8, Case No. 976 - Malicious Mischief

Kowall, Joachim
1876 Sept 4, Case No. 955 - Threats

LaBreuner, Albert
1879 Jan 13, Case No. 1302 - Robbery

Lackey, Samuel
1870 Oct 8, Case No. 436 - Burglary with intent to Rob

Lambie, Calvin
1874 Oct 15, Case No. 733 - Keeping & Exhibiting Gaming Tables

Lamper, W J
1878 Jan 13, Case No. 1299 - Threats

Lancaster, Samuel
1866 Mar 23, Case No. 235 - Gambling; 1866 Mar 23, Case No. 236 - Gambling; 1866 Mar 23, Case No. 237 - Gambling; 1866 Mar 23, Case No. 238 - Gambling; 1866 Mar 23, Case No. 239 - Gambling; 1866 Mar 23, Case No. 240 - Gambling; 1866 Mar 23, Case No. 241 - Gambling; 1866 Mar 23, Case No. 242 - Gambling;

1866 Mar 23, Case No. 243 - Gambling

Lane, Anne
1875 Nov 20, Case No. 857 - Peace warrant

Lane, Edward
1870 Oct 8, Case No. 433 - Larceny

Lane, Thomas
1873 Oct 9, Case No. 627 - Assault with intent to kill and murder

Langford, A G
1877 Feb 20, Case No. 1040 - Contempt

Larkin, Patrick H
1868 May 6, Case No. 349 -

Larmie, Calvert
1870 June 20, Case No. 424 Keeping Gambling Room

Laswell, B F
1878 Sept 27, Case No. 1285 - Contempt

Latta, James
1862 Aug 26, Case No. 95 - Larceny; bef 1862, Case No. 94 - Larceny

Laurence, Edward M
1876 Sept 6, Case No. 970 - Burglary

Lawrence, Ranesford
bef 1862, Case No. 31 - Treason etc.

Lee, T J
1875 Oct 18, Case No. 851 - Contempt

Leighton, Harry
1875 Apr 8, Case No. 766 - Murder

Leischining, Charles
1874 June 1, Case No. 695 - Contempt

Lenny, Phillip
1876 Apr 13, Case No. 908 - Assault with intent to murder; 1876 Apr 13, Case No. 909 - Assault with intent to kill

Leonard, Emma
1866 Dec 6, Case No. 267 - Larceny

Levy, Joseph
1877 Apr 21, Case No. 1055 - Larceny; 1877 Jan 15, Case No. 1015 - False Pretenses

Lewis, James
1879 Jan 13, Case No. 1306 - Larceny

Lewis, Jerre
1875 Apr 25, Case No. 842 - Assault with intent to kill

Lewis, Lemuel N
1866 Dec 12, Case No. 283 - Robbery

Lewis, William
1875 Mar 26, Case No. 752 -

Assault; 1877 Sept 7, Case No. 1130 - Larceny

Leyar, Abram
1873 Apr 12, Case No. 551 - Larceny

Lightner, Hiram
1866 Dec 8, Case No. 274 - Larceny; 1866 Dec 8, Case No. 275 - Larceny

Liles, Abraham
1870 Oct 8, Case No. 434 - Larceny

Lock, Robert H
1879 Jan 13, Case No. 1319 - False Pretenses

Locknane, J M
1863 Mar 10, Case No. 115 -

Londoner, Wolfe
1874, Case No. 696 - Contempt

Lonneberg, Frank
1871 June 15, Case No. 456 - Embezzlement; 1871 June 15, Case No. 457 - Embezzlement

Loomer, Timothy D
1877 Jan 15, Case No. 1016 - Making and paying fictitious note

Lopez, Jose Maria
1868 Oct 9, Case No. 361 - Larceny

Lopez, Maria
1868 Oct 9, Case No. 360 - Larceny

Lotts, Frederick
1872 Oct 7, Case No. 514 - Manslaughter, change of venue from Lake Co

Lowe, J W
1879 Jan 13, Case No. 1320 - Arson

Lowry, William
1866 Dec 6, Case No. 262 - Larceny

Lusigna, Mary
bef 1865, Case No. 152 - Larceny

Lydle, Giles
1871 Jan 4, Case No. 445 - Murder

Lyon, Cornelius
1866 Nov 22, Case No. 257 - Murder

Lyons, Wallis
1878 Jan 18, Case No. 1171 - Burglary

Lyord, James
1866 Dec 8, Case No. 277 - Larceny

MacDonald, Daniel
1875 Sept 18, Case No. 819 - Larceny

Mackey, Richard
1870 Dec 14, Case No. 444 - Murder

Mafais, Viola
1876 June 30, Case No. 937 - Concealing birth of a bastard infant

Maginty, Charles
1873 Oct 8, Case No. 621 - Assault with intent to rape

Mailhouse, Julius
1876 Apr 8, Case No. 892 - Obtaining goods and money under false pretenses

Mailhouse, Julius
1876 Apr 8, Case No. 893 - Larceny

Malroney, Daniel
1863 Mar 3, Case No. 100 - Riot; 1863 Mar 3, Case No. 104 - Larceny

Manhart, Charles
1872 Apr 18, Case No. 510 - Murder

Mann, Emma
1863 Mar 3, Case No. 108 - Keeping Bawdy House

Manning, Frank
1875 Sept 11, Case No. 847 - Larceny

Manning, George
1877 Jan 18, Case No. 1033 - False Pretenses

Manning, James
1875 Sept 11, Case No. 847 - Larceny

Manning, John
1878 Sept 13, Case No. 1275 - Larceny

Marah, Frank O
1875 Sept 25, Case No. 843 - Assault with intent to kill

Mariner, Robert Lee
1866 Mar 21, Case No. 209 - Gambling; 1866 Mar 21, Case No. 210 - Gambling

Marix, Mayer Martin
1877 Jan 18, Case No. 1026 - Abortion

Markham, V D
1874 Dec 16, Case No. 684 - Contempt

Markis, Charles H
1873 Oct 9, Case No. 632 - Larceny

Marron, Joseph
1877 Jan 12, Case No. 997 - Burglary

Marston, Hiram P
1878 Sept 9, Case No. 1267 - Murder

Martin, Barney
1874 Sept 17, Case No. 709 - Larceny

Martin, Charles
1878 Jan 10, Case No. 1172 - Larceny

Martin, John H
1874, Case No. 697 - Contempt

Martin, John W
1870 June 17, Case No. 407 -

Assault with intent to kill; 1872 Oct 10, Case No. 517 - Larceny

Martin, Robert
1879 Jan 15, Case No. 1331 - Larceny

Martin, Thomas
1873 Apr 12, Case No. 554 - Larceny

Martinez, Santez
1866 Nov 22, Case No. 258 - Murder

Marwell, John
bef 1862, Case No. 55 - Treason, etc.

Mason, Thomas
1873 Oct 7, Case No. 616 - Larceny

Masswone, Carry
1879 Apr 15, Case No. 1342 - Threats

Mastison, Thomas
1879 Apr 21, Case No. 1354 - Assault

Mathews, David
1877 Sept 11, Case No. 1143 - Larceny

Mathias, J H
1874 May 25, Case No. 690 - Contempt

Matthew, John W
1865 Dec 6, Case No. 154 - Habeas Corpus

Mauff, August
1876 Apr 13, Case No. 911 - Larceny

Mauff, Edward
1876 Apr 13, Case No. 911 - Larceny

Maulding, T F
1875 May 28, Case No. 689 - Contempt

Maxwell, Evan J
1879 Jan 13, Case No. 1321 - Assault; 1879 Mar 1, Case No. 1338 - Threats

May, Samuel
1876 Sept 5, Case No. 958 - Threats

Maynard, David P
1874 Apr 8, Case No. 647 - Larceny; 1874 Apr 8, Case No. 648 - Larceny

McBride, Robert A
1865 Dec 20, Case No. 189 - Larceny

McBride, Thomas
bef 1862, Case No. 79 - Grand Larceny

McCall, R D
1876 June 20, Case No. 936 - Larceny

McCall, Robert
1876 Sept 13, Case No. 987 - Larceny

McCarty, L
1873 Mar 21, Case No. 592 - Contempt

McCarty, Leander
1875 Sept 21, Case No. 839 - Contempt

McCleary, Comfort
1862 Aug 26, Case No. 95 - Larceny; bef 1862, Case No. 94 - Larceny

McCleary, Daniel
1862 Nov 5, Case No. 96 - Arson

McClish, Stewart
1874 Sept 5, Case No. 701 - Murder (from Lake County)

McClosky, George W
bef 1862, Case No. 56 - Treason, etc.

McComb, Robert
1863 Mar 3, Case No. 106 - Larceny

McConnell, Henry
1879 Jan 13, Case No. 1306 - Larceny

McCorkle, Andrew J
1877 Sept 11, Case No. 1149 - False Pretenses

McCormick, Isaac
1877 Dec 31, Case No. 1191 - Threats

McCoy, Hugh
1876 Sept 13, Case No. 980 - Larceny; 1876 Sept 13, Case No. 981 - Larceny

McCoy, Nathan
1874 Apr 8, Case No. 661 - Burglary

McCray, John
1863 Mar 3, Case No. 102 - Assault to kill

McCrury, Nelson
1865 Dec 16, Case No. 176 - Larceny

McCune, Joseph
1879 Jan 13, Case No. 1322 - Assault

McDonald, William
1878 Sept 9, Case No. 1243 - Cruelty to animals

McElliott, James
1877 Sept 7, Case No. 1125 - Assault

McFate, Wm
bef 1862, Case No. 76 - Passing counterfeit gold dust

McGinnis, Patrick H
1878 Sept 13, Case No. 1276 - Larceny; 1878 Sept 9, Case No. 1261 - Forgery; 1878 Sept 9, Case No. 1262 - Larceny

McKenna, J F
1877 May 18, Case No. 1105 - Appeal

McKenney, Frank
1879 Apr 21, Case No. 1359 - Adultery

McKinney, Cornelius C
1878 Sept 9, Case No. 1261 - Forgery

McKlee, Joel
bef 1862, Case No. 41 - Treason, etc.

McLarren, M H
1877 Apr 21, Case No. 1050 - Forgery

McLaughlin, A
1865 Dec 19, Case No. 169 - Larceny

McLean, Thomas
1863 Mar 3, Case No. 105 - Larceny

McMann, Henry et al
1877 Jan 12, Case No. 1006 - Larceny

McNamara, Barney
1878 Aug 28, Case No. 1234 - Threats

McNamara, Mary
1878 Sept 13, Case No. 1273 - Disturbing the Peace

McTurke, James
1874 Apr 10, Case No. 676 - Assault with intent to kill and murder

Meaney, John
1870 Oct 8, Case No. 431 - Larceny

Meek, Cornell
bef 1862, Case No. 54 - Treason, etc.

Merchant, John
1878 Apr 22, Case No. 1232 - Contempt

Merrick, Duncan
1874, Case No. 698 - Contempt

Mers, John S
bef 1862, Case No. 21 - Treason etc.

Mers, Samuel
bef 1862, Case No. 42 - Treason, etc.

Mers, William L
bef 1862, Case No. 36 - Treason, etc.

Metzner, Edward H
1878 Sept 9, Case No. 1263 - Burglary

Mexican, name unknown
bef 1862, Case No. 117 -

Mickley, J H
1864 Apr 11, Case No. 139 - Gambling & Keeping Gambling House

Mier, Jacob
1870 Jan 20, Case No. 404 - Larceny

Miller, Charles
1878 Apr 20, Case No. 1226 -
Larceny

Miller, Edward S
1873 Apr 11, Case No. 549 -
Larceny; 1873 Oct 2, Case No. 612
- Larceny

Miller, Katy
1876 Sept 4, Case No. 957 -
Threats

Miller, O H
1871 Oct 13, Case No. 483 -
Contempt

Milsap, Budd
1877 Apr 23, Case No. 1072 -
Assault with intent to murder

Milsap, George
1877 Jan 10, Case No. 1176 - Not a
truc bill

Milsap, George et al
1873 Apr 11, Case No. 544 -
Robbery

Milsap, Sawyer B
1874 Apr 10, Case No. 680 -
Assault with intent to kill

Miltimore, James
1876 Jan 29, Case No. 877 -
Forgery

Minkley, Henry J
1866 Mar 22, Case No. 214 -
Gambling; 1866 Mar 22, Case No.
215 - Gambling; 1866 Mar 22,
Case No. 216 - Keeping Gambling

House; 1866 Mar 22, Case No. 222
- Gambling; 1866 Mar 22, Case
No. 223 - Gambling; 1866 Mar 22,
Case No. 224 - Gambling

Minson, William H
1870 June 17, Case No. 406 -
Larceny

Mitchell, Al
1878 Aug 28, Case No. 1235 -
Threats

Mitchell, Charles
1866 Dec 14, Case No. 292 -
Larceny

Mitchell, Mathew J
1878 Apr 18, Case No. 1218 - no
charge cited; 1878 Jan 13, Case No.
1307 - Larceny

Mitchell, Matt
1877 Jan 15, Case No. 1017 -
Larceny

Moire, Nicholas
bef 1862, Case No. 91 - Selling
liquor to soldiers

Moncrief, John
1877 June 5, Case No. 1117 -
Contempt

Monroe, Charles
1876 Apr 13, Case No. 910 -
Larceny

Monroe, D J
1866 Dec 12, Case No. 284 -
Larceny

Monteith, Evans J
1876 Feb 12, Case No. 884 - Appeal

Moore, Frances
1877 Apr 21, Case No. 1051 - Abduction

Moore, Lewis
1862 Nov 5, Case No. 97 - Larceny

Moore, Mahlan
1863 July 20, Case No. 120 - Petit Larceny

Moore, William H
1876 June 1, Case No. 924 - Contempt

Moore, Wm
1864, Case No. 149 - Peace warrant; 1864 Apr 6, Case No. 131 - Larceny

Morgan, James
1866 Dec 12, Case No. 283 - Robbery

Morgan, Jeremati
1865 Dec 16, Case No. 175 - Obtaining money under false pretenses

Morris, Harry O
1878 Jan 10, Case No. 1166 - Larceny; 1878 Jan 10, Case No. 1167 - Larceny; 1878 Jan 10, Case No. 1168 - Bigamy

Morris, Isaac
1873 Apr 14, Case No. 588 - Gambling

Morrison, James
1873 Oct 9, Case No. 628 - Assault with intent to kill and murder

Morrison, John
1866 Dec 14, Case No. 288 - Murder

Mortfort, Joseph
1877 Apr 26, Case No. 1099 - Burglary

Moseley, Aaron L
1872 Oct 8, Case No. 515 - Murder

Mosser, Philip
1876 Sept 5, Case No. 959 - Threats

Moyes, David
1877 Apr 26, Case No. 1100 - Larceny

Mulaly, Michael
1864 Apr 6, Case No. 131 - Larceny

Mullen, John S
1872 Oct 10, Case No. 521 - Larceny

Mulvaney, Thomas
1877 Apr 23, Case No. 1073 - Burglary; 1877 Apr 23, Case No. 1074 - Burglary; 1877 Jan 15, Case No. 1020 - Burglary; 1877 Jan 15, Case No. 1021 - Burglary; 1877 Jan 15, Case No. 1022 - Burglary; 1878 Sept 9, Case No. 1264 - Burglary; 1878 Sept 9, Case No. 1265 - Burglary; 1878 Sept 9, Case No. 1266 - Burglary

Munger, J W
1873 Mar 6, Case No. 595 -
Contempt

Munson, Hugh T
1867 Sept 24, Case No. 320 -
Murder

Murphy, Henry
1876 Oct 17, Case No. 991 -
Appeal

Murphy, Jerry
1877 Sept 11, Case No. 1138 -
Arson

Murphy, Laurence C
1873 Apr 11, Case No. 548 -
Larceny

Murphy, May
1875 Apr 10, Case No. 789 -
Malicious Mischief

Murray, John
1871 Jan 4, Case No. 445 - Murder

Murray, William
bef 1862, Case No. 52 - Treason,
etc.

Myers, J H
1873 May 13, Case No. 599 -
Contempt

Myers, Jesse
bef 1862, Case No. 26 - Treason
etc. aka Jesse C Trotter

Myers, John
bef 1862, Case No. 67 - Passing
counterfeit gold dust; bef 1862,
Case No. 68 - Larceny

Myers, Theodore
1871 Oct 4, Case No. 473 -
Murder; 1871 Oct 4, Case No. 474
- Assault with intent to kill

Narrin, John S
1865 Dec 20, Case No. 180 -
Larceny

Narvney, Rosa
1867 Dec 4, Case No. 325 -
Larceny; 1867 Dec 9, Case No. 338
- Larceny

Nassan, John S
1865 Dec 14, Case No. 160 -
Larceny

Nasser, M James
1867 Sept 24, Case No. 320 -
Murder

Neal, William L
1874 Aug 5, Case No. 699 - Appeal

Nealis, James
1877 Apr 10, Case No. 1210 -
Threats

Neeley, N B
1877 Jan 23, Case No. 1041 -
Contempt

Neff, Joseph
1879 Apr 15, Case No. 1341 -
Threats

Nelson, Harris
1866 Dec 8, Case No. 270 -
Larceny

Nelson, John
1868 Oct 9, Case No. 355 -
Burglary; 1869 May 6, Case No.
375 - Larceny

Nevil, Samuel E
1873 Apr 14, Case No. 585 -
Aiding in Keeping and Gambling
and Playing at Game

Newark, Herr
1870 June 20, Case No. 420 -
Keeping Gambling Tenement

Nichols, H J Wm
1879 Jan 21, Case No. 1334 -
Contempt

Niece, Frank
1866 Mar 21, Case No. 200 -
Gambling; 1866 Mar 21, Case No.
201 - Gambling; 1866 Mar 21,
Case No. 208 - Gambling; 1866
Mar 21, Case No. 212 - Gambling;
1866 Mar 21, Case No. 218 -
Gambling

North, Joseph
bef 1862, Case No. 74 - Passing
counterfeit gold dust; bef 1862,
Case No. 83 - Assault with intent
to kill

Northouse, Frances
1875 Sept 18, Case No. 820 -
Larceny

Norwood, Talmadge C
1879 Jan 13, Case No. 1308 -
Larceny

Nunnelly, William
bef 1862, Case No. 58 - Treason,
etc.

Nye, John A
1876 Apr 4, Case No. 926 -
Contempt

O'Brien, John
1875 Apr 9, Case No. 893 -
Larceny

O'Connors, George
1874 Apr 10, Case No. 679 -
Adultery

Offutt, Mark
1865 Dec 16, Case No. 170 -
Murder

Oliver, John B
1876 Jan 29, Case No. 878 -
Larceny

Olson, Nils P
1878 Feb 6, Case No. 1204 -
Contempt

O'Marak, Frank
1875 Sept 25, Case No. 843 -
Assault

O'Neal, James
1874 Sept 17, Case No. 707 -
Larceny

Orr, Edward L
1877 Sept 7, Case No. 1126 -
Larceny

Ortman, J N
1878 Sept 9, Case No. 1244 -
Larceny

Osgood, Nannie
1878 Jan 10, Case No. 1178 - Not a true bill

Osgood, Samuel
1878 Jan 10, Case No. 1178 - Not a true bill

Oymumes, A C
1870 Oct 8, Case No. 428 - Larceny

Page, John
1877 Sept 12, Case No. 1151 - Forgery

Patrick, Albert
1866 Dec 12, Case No. 285 - Larceny; 1866 Dec 14, Case No. 293 - Larceny

Patrick, George
1870 Oct 8, Case No. 440 - Murder; 1870 Oct 8, Case No. 441 - Murder; 1870 Oct 8, Case No. 442 - Accessory before the fact to murder

Patrick, Henry
1870 Oct 8, Case No. 443 - Accessory after the fact to murder; 1873 Oct 11, Case No. 638 - Perjury; 1874 Apr 9, Case No. 665 - Perjury

Payne, Joseph
1864, Case No. 151 - Gambling; 1864 Apr 13, Case No. 141 - Gambling

Peabody, Henry
1874 Apr 9, Case No. 670 - Larceny

Peabody, John
1878 Oct 2, Case No. 1281 - Contempt

Perjin, Abraham
1865 Dec 20, Case No. 188 - Larceny

Perring, ___
1863 Nov 4, Case No. 123 - Larceny

Peters, Mary E
bef 1862, Case No. 155 - Habeas Corpus

Peters, Stephen et al
bef 1862, Case No. 155 - Habeas Corpus

Petzke, William
1878 Aug 28, Case No. 1236 - Threats; 1879 Jan 9, Case No. 1294 - Threats

Pflayer, Fred
1876 Sept 4, Case No. 960 - Threats

Pickell, John J
1876 May 27, Case No. 922 - Contempt

Pier, Samuel
1867 Dec 9, Case No. 333 - Larceny

Pierce, Gilbert H
1872 Oct 11, Case No. 535 -
Keeping Gambling Establishment

Pierce, Harkin
1879 Apr 21, Case No. 1358 -
Burglary

Pierce, Henry S
1869 Oct 7, Case No. 393 -
Larceny

Plato, William
1864 Apr 13, Case No. 144 -
Gambling

Porter, Charles H
bef 1862, Case No. 66 - Murder;
bef 1862, Case No. 73 -
Manslaughter

Porter, Henry
1864 Apr 13, Case No. 143 -
Gambling

Porter, Leonard L
1877 Sept 11, Case No. 1144 -
Larceny; 1877 Sept 11, Case No.
1145 - Larceny; 1877 Sept 11, Case
No. 1146 - Larceny; 1877 Sept 11,
Case No. 1147 - False Pretenses;
1877 Sept 12, Case No. 1152 -
False Pretenses

Porter, Luther
1864 Apr 7, Case No. 136 -
Burglary & Larceny

Porter, William H
bef 1862, Case No. 19 - Treason,
etc.; bef 1862, Case No. 63 -
Robbery

Price, William
1876 Apr 14, Case No. 918 -
Assault with intent to kill

Price, William
1876 Sept 13, Case No. 988 -
Assault with intent to kill; 1876
Sept 5, Case No. 938 - Assault with
intent to kill

Priller, Maxamillian
1875 May 12, Case No. 808 -
Selling the same land twice

Proctor, Alfred
1875 Apr 15, Case No. 802 -
Assault with a deadly weapon

Racbke, Frederick W
1877 Jan 18, Case No. 1036 -
Embezzlement

Railey, Mark H
bef 1862, Case No. 81 -
Manslaughter

Raitzach, Henry
1879 Apr 21, Case No. 1357 -
Larceny

Ramsford, Charles
1874 Apr 8, Case No. 655 -
Larceny

Rand, William A
1877 Apr 21, Case No. 1052 - False
Pretenses; 1877 Jan 18, Case No.
1031 - False Pretenses

Rappetts, Louis
1875 Sept 18, Case No. 825 -
Larceny

Raymond, William
1873 Oct 7, Case No. 617 - False Pretenses

Ready, William
1871 Oct 4, Case No. 481 - Larceny

Reed, William
1877 Jan 12, Case No. 1007 - Forgery; 1877 Jan 12, Case No. 1008 - Forgery; 1877 Jan 12, Case No. 1009 - Forgery; 1877 Jan 15, Case No. 1024 - Forgery; 1877 Jan 15, Case No. 1025 - Forgery

Reeder, Moses
1875 Sept 25, Case No. 844 - Assault with intent to kill; 1877 Apr 23, Case No. 1075 - Larceny

Reitze, Henry
1878 Sept 20, Case No. 1279 - Contempt

Retchford, James P
1876 June 3, Case No. 920 - Assault & Battery

Revial, Jose R
1871 Oct 4, Case No. 475 - Assault with intent to rape

Reynolds, Benj F
bef 1862, Case No. 2 -

Reynolds, Jack
1875 Apr 9, Case No. 781 - Larceny

Reynolds, James
bef 1862, Case No. 28 - Treason, etc.

Reynolds, John
bef 1862, Case No. 44 - Treason, etc.

Reynolds, Samuel
1876 Sept 4, Case No. 961 - Assault

Rice, Alonzo
1877 June 6, Case No. 1119 - Contempt

Rice, Stephen A
1878 June 4, Case No. 1230 - Contempt

Richardson, James
1874 Apr 8, Case No. 660 - Larceny

Richardson, Robert
1876 Jan 29, Case No. 870 - Larceny

Richville, Robert
1878 Jan 10, Case No. 1173 - Larceny

Rickabaugh, Lon
1870 June 20, Case No. 419 - Common Gambler

Ridgway, Augustus
1870 June 17, Case No. 410 - Assault with intent to kill

Rifal, Albert
1874 Jan 12, Case No. 644 - Appeal

Riley, James
1869 Oct 7, Case No. 395 - Larceny

Ripetto, Louis
1874 Sept 19, Case No. 729 - Obtaining goods under false pretenses

Rippy, Wesley C et al
1877 Dec 6, Case No. 1162 - Contempt

Rivers, James
1867 June 14, Case No. 306 - Larceny

Robbins, Samuel M
bef 1862, Case No. 85 - Bribery

Roberts, Harry
1875 Sept 18, Case No. 816 - alias of Harry Grimet; 1875 Sept 18, Case No. 821 - Burglary, alias Harry Grimet; 1875 Sept 18, Case No. 822 - Burglary, alias Harry Grimet; 1875 Sept 18, Case No. 823 - Burglary, alias Harry Grimet; 1875 Sept 18, Case No. 824 - Burglary, alias Harry Grimet

Roberts, John
1870 Oct 8, Case No. 429 - Larceny

Roberts, One
1870 June 20, Case No. 422 - Keeping Gambling Room

Roberts, Thomas
1870 June 17, Case No. 408 - Larceny

Roberts, William
1876 Jan 29, Case No. 879 - Larceny

Robinson, Amos
1876 Sept 9, Case No. 978 - Larceny

Robinson, Emma
1873 Apr 11, Case No. 541 - Assault with intent to commit murder

Robinson, Joseph F
1866 Mar 24, Case No. 248 - Larceny

Roderijes, Jose
1868 Oct 9, Case No. 360 - Larceny

Rodgers, Juan
1866 Dec 12, Case No. 286 - Assault with intent to kill

Rodinges, Jose
1868 Oct 9, Case No. 363 - Larceny

Roe, James
1875 Oct 8, Case No. 848 -

Roe, Richard
1878 Jan 15, Case No. 1192 - Riot

Rogers, Isaac
1879 Jan 13, Case No. 1324 - Robbery

Rogers, John
1871 Jan 7, Case No. 451 - Larceny; 1875 Apr 6, Case No. 759 - Robbery

Rollins, Richard C
1877 Apr 26, Case No. 1101 -

Larceny; 1877 Apr 24, Case No. 1085 - Larceny

Roper, Samuel
1875 Apr 15, Case No. 803 - Assault & Battery with intent to kill

Ross, James B
1862 Nov 5, Case No. 96 - Arson; 1863 Mar 3, Case No. 101 - Murder; 1875 Sept 18, Case No. 826 - Larceny; 1875 Sept 18, Case No. 827 - Larceny

Ross, Peter
1871 Oct 4, Case No. 479 - Robbery

Rotchford, James P
1875 Dec 27, Case No. 858 - Appeal

Rudy, Israel
1874 Oct 19, Case No. 743 - Contempt

Ruffin, William
1874 Nov 30, Case No. 726 - Assault with intent to murder

Russell, Andrew
1874 Apr 8, Case No. 657 - Larceny

Russell, Edward
1877 Apr 24, Case No. 1084 - Assault; 1878 June 15, Case No. 1212 - Threats; 1879 Jan 13, Case No. 1323 - Assault

Russell, James
1866 Dec 12, Case No. 284 - Larceny; 1867 Dec 4, Case No. 327 - Larceny; 1867 Dec 4, Case No. 328 - Larceny

Ryan, Jack
1875 Sept 18, Case No. 832 - Burglary

Ryan, James
1877 Sept 11, Case No. 1148 - Malicious Mischief

Ryan, John
1871 June 15, Case No. 462 - Larceny; 1871 Oct 4, Case No. 479 - Robbery; 1878 Apr 20, Case No. 1224 - Burglary

Sampson, A S
1874 Oct 26, Case No. 744 - Contempt

Sampson, Amos S
1876 June 30, Case No. 962 - Threats; 1876 June 30, Case No. 939 - Riot

Sampson, Amos S et al
1878 Jan 14, Case No. 1186 - Larceny; 1878 Jan 14, Case No. 1187 - Malicious Mischief

Sarsfield, Thomas
1875 Apr 8, Case No. 769 - Larceny

Schaefer, Charles
1878 Apr 18, Case No. 1219 - Malicious Mischief

Schaefer, Peter
1878 Oct 3, Case No. 1282 -
Contempt

Schon, Henry
1869 May 6, Case No. 376 -
Larceny; 1869 Oct 7, Case No. 380
- Larceny

Schrader, Albert
1873 Oct 7, Case No. 616 -
Larceny

Schuhler, Frederick
1877 Apr 23, Case No. 1077 -
Assault; 1877 Jan 12, Case No.
1010 - Assault with a deadly
weapon

Schulte, John
1874 Apr 9, Case No. 671 -
Larceny

Schwartz, Jas
1879 Jan 6, Case No. 1295 -
Threats

Schworke, Moritz
1874 Apr 8, Case No. 656 -
Larceny

Scott, Clayton
bef 1862, Case No. 12 - Assault
with a Deadly Weapon with Intent
to Kill

Scott, J
1879 Jan 13, Case No. 1301 -
Robbery

Scott, Uriel
bef 1862, Case No. 72 - Passing
counterfeit gold dust

Scott, William H H
1873 Oct 6, Case No. 606 -
Larceny

Scranton, Monroe
1863 Mar 3, Case No. 102 -
Larceny

Scruton, Richard L
1876 June 30, Case No. 963 -
Threats

Sears, J P
1863 Mar 5, Case No. 113 -
Misdemeanor

Sears, Jasper P
1877 Feb 8, Case No. 1042 -
Contempt

Segrone, Daniel L
1878 Sept 9, Case No. 1268 -
Burglary

Selby, W H
1873 May 6, Case No. 596 -
Contempt

Sergeant, C H
1871 Oct 10, Case No. 490 -
Contempt

Seurille, Charles
bef 1862, Case No. 62 - Larceny

Shackelford, Joel W
1876 Jan 13, Case No. 925 -
Contempt

Shanahan, Patrick
1866 Apr 2, Case No. 256 -
Murder

Sharp, Robert
1865 Dec 15, Case No. 165 - Larceny

Shaughnessey, Kate
1876 Apr 13, Case No. 895 - Adultery & Fornication

Shaw, Samuel
1863 Nov 4, Case No. 124 -

Shea, Dennis
1878 Apr 18, Case No. 1220 - Disturbing the Peace

Sheriff of Arapahoe Co
1875 June 7, Case No. 809 - Contempt

Sheriff of El Paso County
1874, Case No. 731 - Contempt; 1874 June 1, Case No. 694 - Contempt

Sheriff, Burt P
1874 Sept 19, Case No. 725 - Assault with intent to rape

Sherron, Charles
1874 Sept 17, Case No. 704 - Larceny

Shields, John
1879 Jan 13, Case No. 1311 - Larceny

Shields, Patrick
1866 Dec 8, Case No. 272 - Larceny; 1866 Dec 8, Case No. 273 - Burglary

Shields, Thomas
1877 Apr 26, Case No. 1102 -

Larceny; 1877 Apr 26, Case No. 1103 - Larceny

Shirley, John
1868 Oct 9, Case No. 357 - Larceny

Shoemaker, John
1870 Oct 8, Case No. 435 - Larceny

Shull, William
1864 Apr 13, Case No. 147 - Gambling

Shull, Wm
bef 1862, Case No. 9 - Larceny and Conspiracy

Shulte, Eugene B
1867 Dec 11, Case No. 344 - Larceny

Simenton, Thomas
1863 Mar 3, Case No. 109 - Burglary

Simpson, Amos P
1869 Oct 7, Case No. 392 - Assault with intent to kill

Simpson, Chas
1868 May 13, Case No. 353 - alias of Wm Simpson

Simpson, Johnson
1875 Oct 11, Case No. 849 - Contempt

Simpson, Joseph R
1871 Apr 8, Case No. 453 - Riot

Simpson, Pedro A
1871 Apr 8, Case No. 453 - Riot;
1871 Apr 8, Case No. 454 -
Larceny

Simpson, Wm
1868 May 13, Case No. 353 -
Fraudulent voting, alias Chas
Simpson

Sims, Richard D
1873 Apr 14, Case No. 583 -
Keeping Gambling Room

Skillian, William
1876 Oct 25, Case No. 992 -
Assault with intent to kill

Slater, M H
1878 Oct 20, Case No. 1280 -
Contempt

Slocum, Thomas J
1868 May 6, Case No. 351 -
Obtaining money under false
pretenses

Smith, Austin
1878 Sept 10, Case No. 1278 -
Contempt

Smith, Benj F
1868 Jan 15, Case No. 345 -
Contempt; 1868 Jan 15, Case No.
346 - Contempt

Smith, Charles
1874 Sept 24, Case No. 728 -
Assault with intent to rape

Smith, Charles J
1877 Apr 26, Case No. 1099 -
Burglary

Smith, Charles W
bef 1862, Case No. 80 - Grand
Larceny

Smith, Frank R
1877 May 17, Case No. 1108 -
Contempt

Smith, Frederick
1873 June 13, Case No. 591 -
Contempt

Smith, Henry
1875 Sept 18, Case No. 829 -
Larceny

Smith, Isaac N
1876 Apr 14, Case No. 855 -
Embezzlement; 1876 Apr 14, Case
No. 856 - Embezzlement

Smith, Jeremiah
1874 Apr 8, Case No. 664 -
Larceny; 1874 Sept 17, Case No.
705 - Larceny

Smith, John
1869 May 6, Case No. 374 -
Larceny; 1878 Apr 20, Case No.
1225 - Larceny

Smith, L K
1874, Case No. 687 - Contempt

Smith, Laf
1875 Apr 10, Case No. 793 -
Assault & Battery with intent to
kill

Smith, Robert
1873 Apr 14, Case No. 560 -
Playing at game for money

Smith, Simon G
1879 Jan 13, Case No. 1309 - Larceny

Smith, W Frank
1877 Feb 10, Case No. 1043 - Contempt

Smith, William
1875 Apr 9, Case No. 780 - Robbery

Smith, William H
1867 Dec 2, Case No. 321 - Murder

Smith, William L
1876 Apr 13, Case No. 912 - Assault with intent to kill

Smithson, H C
1878 Sept 27, Case No. 1286 - Contempt

Smythe, Hugh
1867 Dec 4, Case No. 326 - Larceny

Snider, John
1876 Apr 14, Case No. 919 - Assault & Battery

Snyder, A J et al
1863 Mar 10, Case No. 116 -

Snyder, Andrew J
1862 Aug 27, Case No. 90 - Assault with intent to kill

Snyder, George H
1877 Jan 15, Case No. 1018 - Assault

Sour, Nicholas
1865 Dec 16, Case No. 171 - Obtaining money under false pretenses

Sowers, Baddy
1872 Oct 10, Case No. 530 - Common Gambler

Spence, George B
1875 Apr 9, Case No. 782 - Larceny

Spencer, Charles
1864 Apr 13, Case No. 146 - Gambling

Splain, Timothy
1874 Sept 23, Case No. 718 - Larceny; 1874 Sept 23, Case No. 719 - Larceny

Spotswood, Robert
1873 May 7, Case No. 597 - Contempt

Sprague, Sever H
1867 June 17, Case No. 313 -

St Clair, Harry
1869 Oct 7, Case No. 394 - Obtaining goods under false pretenses

Staderman, Chas G
1877 June 5, Case No. 1118 - Contempt

Stancliffe, Irwin
1878 Jan 14, Case No. 1189 - Not a true bill

Stanley, John G
1879 Apr 8, Case No. 1338 -
Threats

Stanley, Mary E
1875 Apr 10, Case No. 791 -
Cohabitation; 1875 Apr 12, Case
No. 800 - Obtaining money under
false pretenses; 1875 Apr 12, Case
No. 801 - False Pretenses

Stanton, Fred J
1877 Sept 19, Case No. 1157 -
Contempt

Stanton, Frederick J
1865 Dec 13, Case No. 158 -
Assault with intent to kill

Stern, George
1878 Jan 14, Case No. 1190 - Not a
true bill

Stevens, Charles H
1865 Dec 20, Case No. 182 - False
Pretenses

Stevens, John
1866 Dec 12, Case No. 280 -
Larceny

Steward, Edward
1869 Jan 21, Case No. 364 -
Larceny; 1869 Jan 21, Case No.
365 - Larceny

Stokes, John
1877 Oct 5, Case No. 1158 -
Contempt

Stone, Addison F
bef 1862, Case No. 13 - Larceny;

bef 1862, Case No. 49 - Treason,
etc.; bef 1862, Case No. 64 -
Larceny

Stone, H
1866 Mar 27, Case No. 250 -
Murder; 1866 Mar 27, Case No.
251 - Murder

Stone, Timothy
1873 Oct 8, Case No. 631 -
Larceny

Story, Wm
bef 1862, Case No. 9 - Larceny and
Conspiracy

Stratton, George
1879 Jan 15, Case No. 1332 -
Murder

Straus, Jacob
1875 Sept 18, Case No. 828 -
Larceny

Strausburg, Henry
1878 Sept 9, Case No. 1269 -
Forgery

Strause, Jacob
1875 Apr 8, Case No. 768 -
Larceny

Strong, James
bef 1862, Case No. 6 - Larceny &
Receiving Stolen Goods

Stubblefield, David
1879 Jan 13, Case No. 1310 -
Murder

Sullivan, Daniel
1879 Jan 13, Case No. 1302 - Robbery

Sullivan, Dennis
1872 Oct 10, Case No. 531 - Larceny; 1872 Oct 10, Case No. 532 - Assault with intent to commit murder

Sumes, G G
1874 May 30, Case No. 693 - Contempt

Sutherland, H C
1879 Jan 13, Case No. 1325 - Forgery

Swan, William B
1877 Jan 12, Case No. 1007 - Forgery; 1877 Jan 12, Case No. 1008 - Forgery; 1877 Jan 15, Case No. 1024 - Forgery; 1877 Jan 15, Case No. 1025 - Forgery

Sym, Walter
1878 Jan 10, Case No. 1171 - Burglary

Talbot, James
1867 June 14, Case No. 303 - Larceny

Talbot, Robert
1874 Oct 20, Case No. 738 - Contempt

Tangley, Charles
1862 Aug 26, Case No. 87 - Burglary

Taylor, George
1873 Apr 14, Case No. 587 - Gambling

Taylor, George A
1878 Jan 14, Case No. 1188 - Assault with intent to murder

Taylor, Robert
1873 Oct 9, Case No. 625 - Larceny; 1875 Apr 9, Case No. 783 - Larceny

Taylor, William
1876 June 30, Case No. 940 - Larceny

Ten Eyke, Charles S
bef 1862, Case No. 77 - Passing counterfeit gold dust

Tesch, Carl
1878 Jan 14, Case No. 1190 - Not a true bill

Tesch, Robert
1878 Jan 14, Case No. 1190 - Not a true bill

Thatcher, Samuel
1867 Dec 11, Case No. 342 - Gambling; 1867 June 17, Case No. 315 - Keeping Gambling device; 1870 June 20, Case No. 415 - Keeping Gambling Tenement; 1872 Oct 11, Case No. 533 - Keeping Gambling Establishment; 1878 Dec 11, Case No. 341 - Gambling

Thomas, C R
bef 1862, Case No. 70 - Passing counterfeit gold dust

Thomas, David
1874 Sept 17, Case No. 704 - Larceny; 1874 Sept 23, Case No. 716 - Forgery; 1874 Sept 23, Case No. 717 - Forgery

Thomas, John
1877 Sept 5, Case No. 1154 - Threats

Thompson, Aleck
1877 May 17, Case No. 1109 - Contempt

Thompson, Ira
1873 Apr 12, Case No. 552 - Assault with intent to commit murder; 1873 Jan 22, Case No. 645 - Appeal

Thompson, John
1874 Apr 8, Case No. 651 - Burglary

Thune, Robert
1874 Apr 8, Case No. 662 - Larceny

Tiffin Gold and Silver Mining Company
1874 Sept 7, Case No. 702 - Change of Venue from Summit Co

Tilford, George
1877 Jan 15, Case No. 1023 - Larceny

Tilton, John M
1872 Jan 4, Case No. 498 - Larceny

Tipton, William
bef 1862, Case No. 60 - Treason, etc.

Tomlinson, Edw H
1874 Sept 28, Case No. 710 - Forgery

Trask, Frank
1873 Oct 9, Case No. 626 - Larceny; 1873 Oct 9, Case No. 630 - Larceny

Triplett, Henry
1874 Apr 9, Case No. 667 - Larceny; 1874 Nov 30, Case No. 711 - Larceny; 1874 Sept 2, Case No. 713 - Burglary; 1874 Sept 23, Case No. 714 - Burglary

Trotter, Jesse C

bef 1862, Case No. 26 - alias of Jesse Myers
Trout, George
1877 Sept 7, Case No. 1134 - Murder

Tucker, John C
1875 Mar 26, Case No. 752 - Assault

Tunnell, E A
1877 Sept 4, Case No. 1156 - Contempt

Turner, Harriet
1874 Oct 12, Case No. 737 - Contempt

Tuttle, Edward
1870 Jan 20, Case No. 405 - Larceny

Twine, Robert
1877 Apr 23, Case No. 1076 - Larceny

Tyler, John
1873 Oct 6, Case No. 605 - Larceny

Tynan, James
1879 Jan 2, Case No. 1207 - Contempt

Umerselles, George
1867 June 14, Case No. 310 - Larceny

Vail, Edward
1869 May 7, Case No. 384 - Larceny; 1869 May 7, Case No. 385 - Larceny; 1869 May 7, Case No. 386 - Larceny; 1874 Apr 8, Case No. 650 - Larceny

Vail, Willis
1875 Sept 21, Case No. 838 - Larceny

VanCamp, Warren
1877 Dec 1, Case No. 1160 - Larceny, change of venue from Boulder Co; 1877 Dec 1, Case No. 1161 - Larceny

VanEndert, Edw
1865 Dec 20, Case No. 185 - Larceny

Vaugh, William
1873 Nov 25, Case No. 642 - no charges listed

Vaughan, Champion
1878 Oct 15, Case No. 1282 - Contempt

Vigil, Maximo
1866 Dec 12, Case No. 287 - Murder

Vogas, August
1871 June 15, Case No. 469 - Riot; 1865 Dec 16, Case No. 172 - Assault with attempt to kill; 1873 Oct 10, Case No. 636 - Larceny; 1873 Oct 11, Case No. 637 - Forgery; 1873 Oct 8, Case No. 624 - Larceny; 1874 Apr 9, Case No. 666 - Forgery; 1876 Jan 29, Case No. 882 - Perjury; 1877 Sept 7, Case No. 1127 - Cruelty to animals

Wade, Thomas
1872 Oct 10, Case No. 527 - Common Gambler

Wagner, Augustus
1865 Dec 16, Case No. 171 - Obtaining money under false pretenses

Walker, John
1879 Jan 13, Case No. 1328 - Assault

Walker, Thomas
1877 Apr 26, Case No. 1104 - Assault with intent to murder

Walker, William H
1876 Apr 4, Case No. 921 - Contempt

Wall, Jacob
1865 Dec 21, Case No. 194 - Larceny

Wallace, John L
bef 1862, Case No. 59 - Treason, etc.

Walsh, James B
1874 Feb 25, Case No. 646 - Appeal

Wanless, John
bef 1862, Case No. 84 - Extortion

Ward, Augustus
1879 Jan 6, Case No. 1296 - Threats

Ward, Charles R
1866 Mar 22, Case No. 217 - Keeping Gaming House; 1866 Mar 22, Case No. 219 - no charge listed; 1867 Dec 11, Case No. 342 - Gambling; 1870 June 20, Case No. 418 - Keeping Gambling Rooms; 1873 Apr 14, Case No. 584 - Keeping Gambling Room; 1873 Oct 11, Case No. 534 - Keeping Gambling Establishment; 1878 Dec 11, Case No. 341 - Gambling

Warner, William
1874 Oct 19, Case No. 712 - Burglary

Warren, Edmund
1877 Sept 7, Case No. 1133 - Larceny

Watkins, Leonard A
1878 Apr 23, Case No. 1231 -

Watson, Coggsville J
1879 Apr 21, Case No. 1355 - Assault; 1879 Apr 21, Case No. 1356 - Robbery

Watson, James F
1877 Feb 9, Case No. 1044 - Contempt

Watters, Thomas
1875 Apr 6, Case No. 761 - Larceny

Wearer, Louis
1870 Oct 8, Case No. 430 - Larceny; 1871 Jan 7, Case No. 448 - Larceny

Webb, James
1871 Oct 21, Case No. 486 - Larceny

Webber, Frank
1874 Oct 28, Case No. 747 - Contempt

Webster, Daniel
1866 Dec 14, Case No. 295 - Involuntary Manslaughter

Weiler, William Harry
1878 Aug 28, Case No. 1287 - Threats

Weimsky, Henry
1876 Jan 29, Case No. 881 -
Larceny

Weir, T G
1875 Sept 18, Case No. 826 -
Larceny; 1875 Sept 18, Case No.
827 - Larceny

Wells, Fannie
1863 Mar 3, Case No. 107 - Bawdy
House

Weloty, William
1873 Apr 10, Case No. 539 -
Bigamy

West, Frank
1875 Apr 6, Case No. 760 -
Larceny

Whalen, James
1874 Apr 8, Case No. 653 -
Larceny; 1874 Apr 8, Case No. 654
- Burglary

Wharton, John
1876 Sept 5, Case No. 941 -
Fornication

Wharton, Lillie
1876 Sept 5, Case No. 941 -
Fornication

Wheeler, Edward P
1875 Sept 18, Case No. 830 -
Embezzlement and Larceny;
1876 Jan 29, Case No. 880 -
Embezzlement

White, A J
1877 Apr 21, Case No. 1053 - False

Pretenses; 1877 Apr 21, Case No.
1054 - False Pretenses

White, Douglas
1879 Jan 13, Case No. 1327 -
Larceny

White, George
1872 Jan 4, Case No. 499 - Larceny

White, Jack
1867 June 14, Case No. 305 -
Assault with intent to rob

White, James T
1866 Mar 24, Case No. 249 -
Gambling

White, James Y
1866 Mar 24, Case No. 244 -
Gambling

White, John F
1874 Apr 9, Case No. 668 -
Larceny;
1876 Sept 5, Case No. 942 -
Assault with intent to rob

White, Robert
1875 Sept 18, Case No. 832 -
Burglary

Whittaker, George
1878 Sept 13, Case No. 1277 -
Burglary

Wick, Daniel
1879 Jan 13, Case No. 1313 -
Larceny

Wiggins, Marion
1877 Apr 26, Case No. 1100 -
Larceny

Wilcox, P P
1862 Aug 27, Case No. 92 - Assault & Battery; 1862 Nov 5, Case No. 99 - Palpable omission of duty; 1863 Mar 5, Case No. 114 - Misdemeanor

Wilder, William H
1876 Feb 1, Case No. 883 - Aiding Prisoners to Escape

Wiley, Andrew
1878 Sept 9, Case No. 1270 - Assault

Wiley, John R
1878 Sept 9, Case No. 1271 - Robbery

William, Henry J
1874 Oct 26, Case No. 745 - Contempt

Williams, Eliza
1879 Apr 21, Case No. 1359 - Adultery

Williams, Howard J
1879 Jan 13, Case No. 1312 - Larceny

Williams, Marshall
1871 Jan 4, Case No. 445 - Murder

Willis, Charles
1871 Oct 4, Case No. 476 - Rape

Willoughby, Edmund A
1875 June 7, Case No. 809 - Contempt; 1875 Sept 18, Case No. 833 - Embezzlement and Larceny

Willson, Thomas
1874 Apr 10, Case No. 674 - False Pretenses

Wilson, A J
bef 1862, Case No. 63 - Robbery

Wilson, Anderson
bef 1862, Case No. 39 - Treason, etc.

Wilson, Andrew J
bef 1862, Case No. 37 - Treason, etc.

Wilson, George
1870 Oct 8, Case No. 438 - Larceny

Wilson, Henry
1873 Oct 8, Case No. 623 - Larceny

Wilson, James
1874 Oct 14, Case No. 740 - Contempt

Wilson, Jane
1879 Jan 8, Case No. 1297 - Threats

Wilson, Marry
1870 Oct 8, Case No. 434 - Larceny

Wilson, Richard
1865 Dec 15, Case No. 166 - Larceny

Wirn, James W
bef 1862, Case No. 71 -

Wise, George W
1875 Sept 15, Case No. 845 - Peace warrant

Wisner, Nathan
1865 Dec 13, Case No. 159 - Larceny; 1865 Dec 20, Case No. 187 - Larceny

Withelm, Wm L
1870 Oct 8, Case No. 487 - Robbery

Witherell, George R
1872 Jan 4, Case No. 492 - Forgery; 1872 Jan 4, Case No. 493 - Larceny

Wixon, H M
1876 Sept 5, Case No. 964 - Threats

Wolf, William
1878 Apr 10, Case No. 1211 - Threats

Wolfil, D Fred
1871 June 15, Case No. 465 - Larceny

Wood, Jane
1879 Jan 13, Case No. 1326 - Malicious Mischief

Wood, John
1870 June 17, Case No. 409 - Larceny

Wood, Mike
1877 Feb 3, Case No. 1045 - Contempt

Wood, Robert
1870 Oct 8, Case No. 487 - Robbery

Woodbury, Samuel
1875 Sept 18, Case No. 831 - Larceny

Woods, Georgie et al
1877 Sept 1, Case No. 1155 - Threats

Woods, Jane
1879 Jan 8, Case No. 1297 - Threats

Woods, Jason
1877 Apr 21, Case No. 1056 - Larceny

Woodward, O H
1874 Oct 12, Case No. 736 - Contempt

Woodward, Ona H
1863 Nov 4, Case No. 122 - Burglary & Larceny; 1869 May 7, Case No. 379 - Receiving stolen goods; 1876 Apr 13, Case No. 913 - Keeping Gambling House

Wooley, Lansing
1874 Sept 19, Case No. 724 - Assault with intent to kill and murder

Work, John C
bef 1862, Case No. 25 - Treason, etc.; bef 1862, Case No. 63 - Robbery

Workman, George
1875 Sept 21, Case No. 836 - Illegal voting

Wortman, George
1874 Oct 16, Case No. 741 - Contempt

Wright, Burwell C
1865 Dec 20, Case No. 181 - False Pretenses

Wright, Charles
1873 Apr 14, Case No. 557 - Keeping Gambling Room; 1873 Apr 14, Case No. 562 - Keeping Gambling Room; 1873 Apr 14, Case No. 578 - Keeping Gambling Room; 1873 Apr 14, Case No. 579 - Keeping Gambling Room; 1873 Apr 14, Case No. 580 - Keeping Gambling Room; 1873 Apr 14, Case No. 581 - Keeping Gaming Tables; 1873 Apr 14, Case No. 582 - Keeping Gambling Room; 1873 Apr 14, Case No. 583 - Keeping Gambling Room; 1875 Apr 10, Case No. 794 - Keeping a Room known as Bank Exchange for Gambling; 1875 Apr 10, Case No. 795 - Playing and betting at cards; 1875 Apr 10, Case No. 796 - Exhibiting Gaming Devices; 1875 Apr 10, Case No. 797 - Exhibiting Gaming Devices; 1875 Apr 10, Case No. 798 - Keeping a Gambling Room; 1873 Apr 14, Case No. 561 - Keeping Gambling Room

Wright, David
1874 Oct 26, Case No. 746 - Contempt

Wright, Elizabeth R
bef 1862, Case No. 11 - Murder

Wright, Eugene E
1872 Apr 5, Case No. 507 - Assault with intent to kill and murder; 1872 Apr 5, Case No. 508 - Escaping from jail; 1872 Jan 4, Case No. 494 - Larceny

Wright, James
1871 Oct 21, Case No. 487 - Assault with intent to commit murder

Yean, Yon
1874 Sept 24, Case No. 721 - Larceny

Young, Peter
1876 Oct 13, Case No. 967 - Larceny; 1876 Sept 5, Case No. 966 - False Pretenses

Young, W H
1874 Apr 11, Case No. 682 - False Pretenses

Young, William H
1873 Oct 10, Case No. 636 - Larceny; 1873 Oct 11, Case No. 637 - Forgery; 1874 Apr 9, Case No. 666 - Forgery; 1874 Apr 10, Case No. 672 - False Pretenses

Younker, Jason T
1876 Oct 13, Case No. 994 - Contempt

www.ingramcontent.com/pod-product-compliance
Lightning Source LLC
Chambersburg PA
CBHW061512040426
42450CB00008B/1578